Hillary

Python
For GCSE Computer Science

Computer programming is great fun. True.
Python is one of the most popular programming languages to learn. Also true!

That's where this CGP book comes in — it's a fantastic step-by-step guide to Python programming. We've packed it with examples, practice questions and coding challenges to get you thinking like a programmer.

There are also answers at the back and a bunch of downloadable Python files for practical on-screen practice. Enjoy!

How to access your free Online Edition

This book includes a free Online Edition to read on your PC, Mac or tablet.
To access it, just go to **cgpbooks.co.uk/extras** and enter this code...

3566 4964 3282 6269

By the way, this code only works for one person. If somebody else has used this book before you, they might have already claimed the Online Edition.

Programming Guide

Contents

Section One — Introduction to Python
What is Python?...2
Installing Python..3
The Shell Window...4
The Editor Window..5
Errors..6
Representing Algorithms...............................9
The Program Design Cycle..........................11

Section Two — Inputs, Outputs and Variables
Hello World!..12
Variables...13
Practice Questions and Activities................15
Getting User Inputs.....................................16
Formatting Outputs.....................................18
Practice Questions and Activities................19
Coding Challenges for Section Two............20

Section Three — Data Types and Operations
Data Types..21
Arithmetic Operators...................................23
Practice Questions and Activities................24
Relational Operators....................................26
Boolean Operators.......................................27
String Handling..29
Practice Questions and Activities................31
Coding Challenges for Section Three..........33

Section Four — if Statements
if Statements..34
else Clause..36
elif Clause...37
Practice Questions and Activities................39
Coding Challenges for Section Four............41

Section Five — Iteration
for Loops..42
Practice Questions and Activities................45
while Loops..46
Practice Questions and Activities................49
Coding Challenges for Section Five.............50

Section Six — Data Structures
Lists..51
Practice Questions and Activities................53
Iterating Through Lists................................54
2D Lists..55
Practice Questions and Activities................57
Tuples...58
Sets...59
Dictionaries..60
Practice Questions and Activities................61
Coding Challenges for Section Six...............62

Section Seven — Subroutines
Subroutines..63
Built-in Subroutines.....................................64
Practice Questions and Activities................66
User-defined Functions................................67
Practice Questions and Activities................69
Global and Local Variables..........................70
Parameters and Return Values....................72
Practice Questions and Activities................73
Modules..74
The Time Module...75
The Random Module....................................76
Turtle Graphics..77
Practice Questions and Activities................79
Coding Challenges for Section Seven..........80

Section Eight — File Handling
Using External Files.....................................81
Reading from Text Files...............................82
Managing External Files..............................84
Writing to Text Files....................................85
Updating and Deleting Content in Text Files.......86
Practice Questions and Activities................87
Coding Challenges for Section Eight...........88

Contents

Section Nine — Making Programs Robust

Validation 89
Regular Expressions 91
Practice Questions and Activities 93
Debugging 94
Exception Handling 95
Practice Questions and Activities 97
Coding Challenges for Section Nine 98

Section Ten — Algorithms and More Coding Challenges

Searching Algorithms 99
Sorting Algorithms 101
Practice Questions and Activities 104
Advanced Coding Challenges 105
Ideas for Advanced Coding Projects 110

Answers 111
Index 125

There are lots of **additional files** for use with this book. These include example Python programs that you'll see on the pages, Python programs that are example answers for questions or challenges and other types of file too (e.g. .txt or .csv).

You can find the **full set of these files** at cgpbooks.co.uk/GCSEPythonExtras

You can also access all of the files by scanning this **QR code**.

Published by CGP

Based on the classic CGP style created by Richard Parsons.

Written by Alex Brown and Paul Clowrey.

Editors: Sammy El-Bahrawy, Christopher Lindle, Megan Mooney and Adam Worster

Reviewers: Oliver Kerr and Shaun Whorton

With thanks to Irfan Amin, Shaun Harrogate, John Leonard and Simon Little for the proofreading.

ISBN: 978 1 78908 862 5

With thanks to Laura Jakubowski and Emily Smith for the copyright research.

Raspberry Pi is a trademark of Raspberry Pi Trading.
Firefox is a trademark of the Mozilla Foundation in the U.S. and other countries.
Linux® is the registered trademark of Linus Torvalds in the U.S. and other countries.
macOS is a trademark of Apple Inc., registered in the U.S. and other countries.
Microsoft® Visual Studio Code® & Windows® are trademarks of the Microsoft group of companies.

Printed by Elanders Ltd, Newcastle upon Tyne.
Clipart from Corel®

Text, design, layout and original illustrations © Coordination Group Publications Ltd (CGP) 2022
All rights reserved.

Photocopying more than one section of this book is not permitted, even if you have a CLA licence.
Extra copies are available from CGP with next day delivery • 0800 1712 712 • www.cgpbooks.co.uk

Section One — Introduction to Python

What is Python?

Learning Objectives

Learning Python takes time, but it's a useful skill to have. So, make some tea, grab a biscuit and we'll dive into the world of programming with Python.

- Learn about the history of Python.
- Understand the purpose of Python.
- Learn about some websites and applications where Python is used.
- Learn about some other uses for Python.

The history of Python

1) It was created in 1991 by Guido van Rossum.
2) The name was taken from "Monty Python's Flying Circus", a classic BBC comedy series.
3) The current version, Version 3, first appeared in 2008 and gets regular updates, e.g. 3.10.1 and 3.10.2.
4) In recent years, it's been adopted by educators around the world as the programming language of choice in the classroom. Python is commonly used with the popular Raspberry Pi computer.

The purpose of Python

1) Python is an open-source, high-level programming language designed to be easy to learn and run on multiple devices.
2) High-level languages use commands based on real languages ("if", "then" and "print") to make them easy to understand. A key aim of Python was to be as simple and accessible as possible.
3) Python is popular with programmers at all levels — from single line programs written in primary schools to the world's biggest streaming services, the language is the same.

Python is a really popular programming language

Python has been used to build websites and applications that are used by billions of people. Some examples include:

- YouTube™ — there's a chance you may have come across this website before...
- Firefox sync server — used to synchronise Firefox web browsers across different devices anywhere in the world.
- Blender — an open source 3D modelling application, used to create CGI and animated films.

Python is used in lots of different settings

1) Software development — from home-made apps to massive platforms used on a global scale.
2) Artificial intelligence — Python is used in machine learning algorithms which enable programs to make choices based on data analysis.
3) Website development — there are many Python tools that can be used to enhance and add interactivity to websites.
4) Simple game development — Python is ideal for creating simple 2D games.

Q1 Visit www.python.org and write down three other practical uses of Python you discover.

Installing Python

Learning Objectives

Python is freely available from a number of sources. This page will tell you everything you need to know about installing your new hobby.

- Understand the purpose of an IDE.
- Understand the purpose of IDLE.
- Learn about where to download Python and how to install it.
- Learn about other ways you can use Python.

Programmers use IDEs for developing programs

1) An Integrated Development Environment (IDE) is a piece of software designed to help programmers write and test their code.
2) IDE software includes editing and compiling tools that format and translate program code into a language the computer can understand and output.
3) Many IDEs provide help as you code, using colours to highlight keywords, errors and help with program structure.
4) There are multiple free and paid-for versions of IDEs that are easily available.

Popular IDE applications for use with Python include IDLE, Microsoft® Visual Studio Code®, PyCharm and Spyder.

Different IDEs may use different colours for highlighting, but you can usually customise them.

Examples in this book use IDLE

- Created by Python, it's a simple IDE application with very few distractions.
- IDLE is ideal for beginners and can be installed for free on any computer.
- It includes an editing window for coding and a Shell window for output (see pages 4-5 for more information about the two windows).

Python can be installed on different operating systems

1) Python 3 can be installed on the following operating systems:
   - Windows® — download and install the executable file.
   - macOS operating system software — download and install the pkg file.
   - UNIX®/Linux® — Python is normally pre-installed, but can also be downloaded from the official site.
   - Raspberry Pi OS — Python is normally pre-installed when using a Raspberry Pi.
2) Once downloaded, open the installation file, and follow the instructions.

Reliable official downloads for all operating systems can be found at www.python.org

It can be easier to code on a computer or laptop as you have a big screen and proper keyboard.

There are other ways to use Python

1) There are downloadable apps that allow code to be written and previewed on mobile devices.
2) There are also websites that allow you to write and test Python code — they're basically online IDEs.
3) Working online means that no software needs to be installed — all you need is an internet connection. However, some sites don't allow programs to be saved.
4) It's a good idea to work and save programs locally on your computer, instead of saving programs online or programming on a mobile device.

Popular browser-based Python applications include Replit, Programiz, trinket and W3Schools.

Dealing with Python(s) could leave you feeling a bit constricted...

Learning anything new can be daunting at first. It's important to take your time and slowly work through these initial pages until it starts making sense. Before long, you'll be happy conversing with snakes.

Section One — Introduction to Python

The Shell Window

Learning Objectives

When you first start, getting programs to work can be frustrating. But worry not, you'll be working out what's wrong and fixing it in no time.

- Understand the purpose of the Shell window and its connection to the Editor.
- Learn how to use the Shell for testing code.
- Understand the limitations of the Shell.

The purpose of the Shell window

1) In this book, you'll see lots of small programs. They're typed into the Editor (see next page) and previewed in the Shell window.
2) The purpose of the Shell is to show you the output of your program. Imagine it's a separate computer screen, just running your program.
3) It displays all outputs from your program. E.g. the result of a calculation, questions that need an input response or a simple pattern made up of characters.

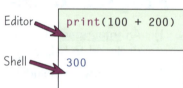

Using the Shell window to instantly test code

1) The programs shown in this book are designed to be written, saved and run within the IDLE Editor.
2) You can also just type into the Shell window and see the response.
3) This is handy for testing lines of code without having to save it first.

EXAMPLE You can instantly see the output of a simple line of code by pressing the return key.

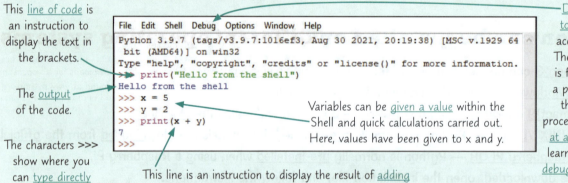

This line of code is an instruction to display the text in the brackets.

The output of the code.

The characters >>> show where you can type directly into the Shell.

Variables can be given a value within the Shell and quick calculations carried out. Here, values have been given to x and y.

This line is an instruction to display the result of adding 5 (x) and 2 (y). The output (7) is shown on the next line.

Debugging tools can be accessed here. The Debugger is for checking a program and the data it's processing, one line at a time. You'll learn more about debugging on p.94.

Now this is a debugging tool.

Using the Shell window has limitations

1) The Shell doesn't save any code, so once closed any code you've typed in is erased.
2) It's only suitable for testing lines of code or very short programs.

Q1 What output is generated from the code shown?

```
>>>a = 10
>>>b = 2
>>>print(a * b)
```

Hope you're not feeling too shellshocked...

Being able to instantly test your code is incredibly useful. Don't panic if things don't work as you expect the first time. Take a look at what you've written and see if you can work out what went wrong.

Section One — Introduction to Python

The Editor Window

Learning Objectives

Code, save, run, repeat... This simple set of steps is what binds all programmers together. Think of it as being a knight with a 'code' to live by.

- Understand the purpose of the Editor window.
- Learn how to create, save and run a new simple program.
- Learn about the tools included in the Editor.

The Editor is used for writing code

The Editor is to used for typing in, editing and saving your code.
1) It allows you to create any number of programs of any size.
2) It provides guidance and formatting help as you code.
3) Files made in the Editor are saved as .py format files.

There are simple steps to create and save a Python file

After opening IDLE, the Shell window (see previous page) normally opens by default.

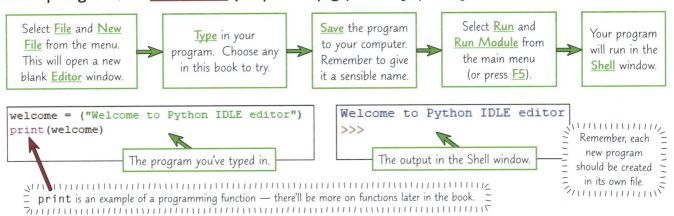

| Select **File** and **New File** from the menu. This will open a new blank Editor window. | **Type** in your program. Choose any in this book to try. | **Save** the program to your computer. Remember to give it a sensible name. | Select **Run** and **Run Module** from the main menu (or press **F5**). | Your program will run in the Shell window. |

```
welcome = ("Welcome to Python IDLE editor")
print(welcome)
```
The program you've typed in.

```
Welcome to Python IDLE editor
>>>
```
The output in the Shell window.

Remember, each new program should be created in its own file.

print is an example of a programming function — there'll be more on functions later in the book.

IDLE Editor has some useful tools

The Editor window within IDLE contains the following features:

- **Auto-indentation** — lines that end in a colon require the next line to be indented. The Editor will do this for you.
- **Code completion tips** — whilst typing, options for completing recognisable functions will appear as guidance.
- **Visual customisation** — you can change the way the Editor looks, including text and background colours and whether line numbers are included.
- **Adding extensions** — these allow extra functionality to be added to IDLE, from new visual options to line-by-line testing.
- **Check Module** — this automatically checks your code for syntax errors (see next page) when you press 'Run Module' and will also prompt you to save the file if it hasn't been saved.

Many new programmers type lines of code and try to save their work, only to find they have typed it all into the Shell window. Sigh. Don't forget to double check which window you're typing into — if you see >>> you're in the Shell window.

"Save me, please, save me! I won't be able to run if you don't..."

Saving your work is very important when working with Python. You won't be able to run your program unless you've already saved it. So, it's good to get into the habit of saving your work whenever you can.

Section One — Introduction to Python

Errors

Learning Objectives

"It's not working, why isn't it working? Oh wait, print only has one n..." Python, like all programming languages, has its own set of rules and breaking them will result in an error.

- Understand what a program error is.
- Understand what a syntax error is.
- Understand what a logic error is.
- Learn some examples of common errors.
- Learn how to tackle errors when they appear.

A lot of what's covered on these pages is a reference for later on when you start encountering errors. Don't worry if it's a bit tricky to get your head around at the moment. You can refer back to this section as you come across errors later in the book.

Errors can stop your program

1) A computer program will stop for two reasons, it's either been programmed to stop, or there's an error that causes it to stop.
2) Until you run it, IDLE has no idea if the code you've written is perfect or full of mistakes, it will simply follow the instructions given.
3) There are two types of program error you need to be aware of — syntax errors and logic errors.

Syntax errors happen when you break the rules

1) The syntax of every programming language is a set of rules.
2) Syntax errors break these rules and so cannot be understood by the computer.

CODE ERRORS

The most common syntax errors are spelling mistakes and incorrectly formatted code. Here are some examples of syntax errors to look out for:

Remember, the * is used to show multiplication.

Functions are case-sensitive — e.g. the print function won't work if written in capitals.

```
PRINT("Error-free coding")
```
```
NameError: name 'PRINT' is not defined
```

Using incorrect characters will cause an error — e.g. mixing bracket types.

```
print("Python can do lots more than display messages"]
```
```
SyntaxError: closing parenthesis ']' does not match opening parenthesis '('
```

Simple mistakes such as using an x instead of an * in a calculation.

```
minutesHour = 60
hoursDay = 24
print("The number of minutes in one day is", minutesHour x hoursDay)
```
```
Syntax Error: invalid syntax
```

Logic errors don't stop a program running

1) A more difficult error to resolve happens when a mistake is made while designing the program.
2) A logic error won't show when the program is run as the program thinks everything is fine.

CODE ERRORS

The program below has been written to calculate the number of days in a year.

The code calculates that 7 × 52 = 364. The maths is correct.

The problem is that our calendar is more complex than this — years actually have 365 or 366 days.

```
daysWeek = 7
weeksYear = 52
print("The number of days in one year is", daysWeek * weeksYear)
```
```
The number of days in one year is 364
```

This is a logic error — the code doesn't break any rules (there are no syntax errors) but it gives an incorrect result, so doesn't work as the programmer intended.

Section One — Introduction to Python

Errors

Common programming error messages to know about

It's useful to know about some common errors so you can avoid them when writing your own code.

There are loads of possible errors you can encounter (don't worry, it's part of learning to code) but here are a few examples to get to grips with.

`SyntaxError: invalid syntax`

The standard syntax error message, it will appear when you break one of Python's rules.

`SyntaxError: expected an indented block`

Indent errors are also syntax errors. This error means there's a missing gap (indent) at the start of a line of code.

`NameError: name 'captain' is not defined`

Variations of this error will appear when variables or other objects are referred to that don't exist.

> Don't worry if these messages don't make sense to you yet. Keep referring back to this section as you work through the book. It'll be here as a reference when you encounter errors

`TypeError: can only concatenate str (not "int") to str`

Variations of this error will appear when incorrect data types are part of a calculation or process.

> `NameError` and `TypeError` are runtime errors. Runtime errors occur when the program is running and comes across something it cannot execute, causing it to stop early. Syntax errors, on the other hand, will prevent the program from running in the first place.

Checking your work will improve your programming

It's easy for errors to creep in when you're programming. Use the basic checklist below as a guide for the sort of mistakes to look out for while writing code.

- [ ] Check the Python functions you've used are spelt correctly.

- [ ] Check you're using lowercase when typing functions. For example, `input` not `INPUT`.

- [ ] Check that any variable names you've created match exactly when used. For example, `daysWeek` and `daysweek` would be two different variable names.

- [ ] Always check the symbols you use. Don't mix brackets or similar characters, such as + and &.

- [ ] Check any use of indentation, especially after an `if` statement or colon.

- [ ] Check that the first value in any list is at index position 0, not 1.

- [ ] Check that you've added colons to the end of `if` statements or loops.

> You won't have come across some of the items on this checklist before. Don't worry if you don't understand them — they will be explained later on.

> This checklist is an example of things to watch out for. Making your own checklist is a good way to ensure you thoroughly go through your work.

Section One — Introduction to Python

Errors

Testing is important for finding and fixing errors

1) It's important to frequently run and test your code as you're writing your program. Testing smaller sections is easier than testing an entire program when trying to find an error.
2) Try following a flowchart, like the one shown below, if a program you're making goes wrong.

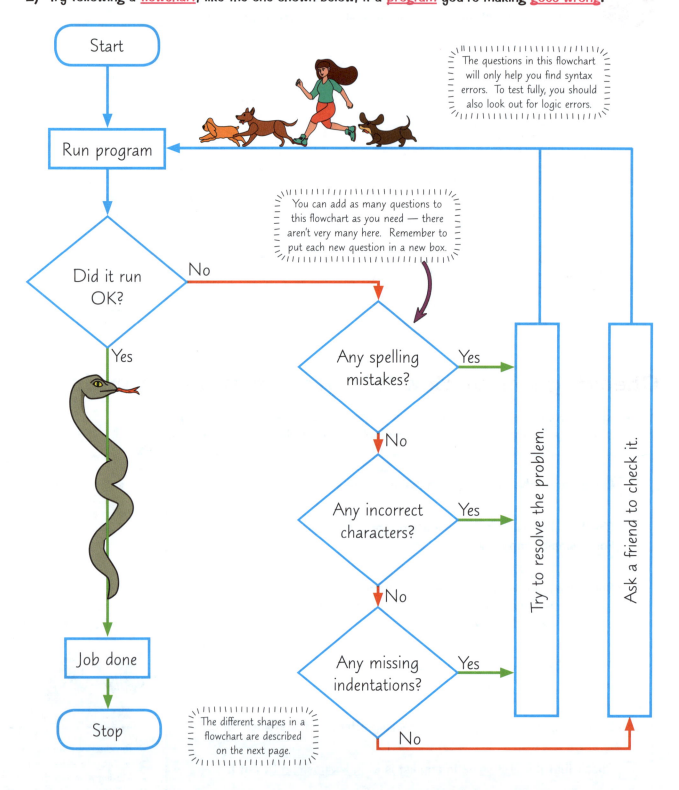

The questions in this flowchart will only help you find syntax errors. To test fully, you should also look out for logic errors.

You can add as many questions to this flowchart as you need — there aren't very many here. Remember to put each new question in a new box.

The different shapes in a flowchart are described on the next page.

Dude, programming is just about, like, going with the flow...

I love flowcharts and by the end of this section, I'm sure you'll love flowcharts too. They're a great way of presenting complex processes logically and, of course, super handy for dealing with errors.

Section One — Introduction to Python

Representing Algorithms

Learning Objectives

Go to fridge... open fridge... take snack... close fridge... eat snack... That's just my routine for getting a midnight snack. Ooooooh, I wonder if I have any cheese...

- Understand what an algorithm is and how one can be represented.
- Understand the purpose of flowcharts.
- Learn about the symbols used in a flowchart.
- Understand the purpose of pseudocode.
- Learn some common pseudocode words.

Algorithms can be created in a number of ways

1) An algorithm is a set of steps or instructions that follow a logical sequence.
2) Algorithms are written to solve a specific problem.
3) They can be represented in a variety of ways:
   - simple sentences
   - a series of logical steps
   - a flowchart diagram
   - code-like pseudocode
   - a high-level language such as Python.

Q1 Write your own short algorithm about making a cup of tea or coffee.

4) Algorithms don't have to be complicated. They can be about something simple like making toast:

Bread in toaster. → Turn on toaster. → Wait until toast is done. → Do the Macarena → Butter toast

Flowcharts use specific symbols

1) A flowchart is used to visualise an algorithm.
2) Different boxes (also known as symbols) are used to represent different commands — specific instructions are written inside them.
3) They are normally created before pseudocode or Python is written.

You might see slight variations in the different boxes used in flowcharts, but some common ones are shown below.

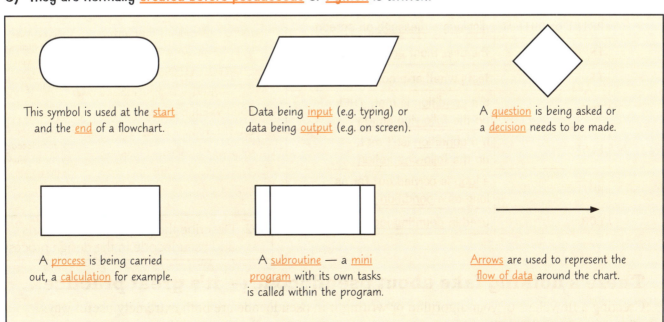

This symbol is used at the start and the end of a flowchart.

Data being input (e.g. typing) or data being output (e.g. on screen).

A question is being asked or a decision needs to be made.

A process is being carried out, a calculation for example.

A subroutine — a mini program with its own tasks is called within the program.

Arrows are used to represent the flow of data around the chart.

Section One — Introduction to Python

Representing Algorithms

Flowcharts are used to see how a program will flow

The best way to see this is to look at an example.

EXAMPLE Create a simple question game program for the question 'What is the capital of France?'.

Here's how it will look if you write it as a logical sequence:

- The computer asks the question
- The user types in their answer
- The computer checks the answer against Paris
- If it's correct, the computer says 'Well done!'
- If it's wrong, the user is re-asked and can guess again.

Now, using the same symbols as on the previous page, the above logical sequence can be created as a flowchart.

Start → Output message: What is the capital of France? → User Input: Type in answer. → Does answer = Paris? → No → Output message: Sorry, try again. (loops back) / Yes → Output message: Well done! → Stop

Writing pseudocode doesn't require a computer

1) Having planned out an algorithm, many programmers then use pseudocode.
2) Pseudocode is a set of instructions in the style of a programming language but using plain English. It uses common coding terms and structure.
3) It's not designed to be run on a computer as there are no specific rules to follow.
4) It's a basic method of program design that can then be easily converted to a real programming language, such as Python.

Although there are no official rules for pseudocode, most exam boards publish their own recommended terms to use.

Common pseudocode keywords

Many of the keywords below are also used in Python, so you'll see them throughout this book:

PRINT or OUTPUT	displays a message on screen
INPUT	the user must enter a response
IF	tests whether a condition is true
THEN	if a condition is met, THEN do the following action
ELSE	if a condition isn't met, do the following action
WHILE	a loop is carried out for as long as a condition is met
FOR	used in counting loop programs

EXAMPLE The same algorithm from above can be created in pseudocode:

OUTPUT("What is the capital of France?")
INPUT user inputs their answer
WHILE answer ≠ "Paris"
    OUTPUT "Sorry, try again"
    INPUT user inputs their answer
END WHILE
OUTPUT "Well done!"

What is the capital of France?
Paris
Well done!

≠ means 'not equal to'.

The green text is the pseudocode and the blue text is the output.

Q2 Describe the purpose of flowcharts and pseudocode in the design process.

There's nothing fake about pseudocode — it's great practice...

Creating a flowchart of your algorithm or writing it in pseudocode are both extremely useful ways of running through the thought processes behind your program before actually using a computer.

The Program Design Cycle

Learning Objectives

Strap on your helmet, it's time to look at the program design cycle. This page will exercise your brain in the same way riding a bicycle exercises your legs.

- Understand the purpose of the program design cycle.
- Learn about the individual cycle elements.
- Learn how you will apply the cycle to your own programming.

The program design cycle applies to projects of any size

1) The purpose of the program design cycle is to break down the process of designing a solution to any problem into manageable parts.
2) Using the cycle helps to reduce errors in a program.
3) Once the cycle is complete, it can begin again, making improvements to the program.
4) This process can be repeated until you are happy that the program is finished.

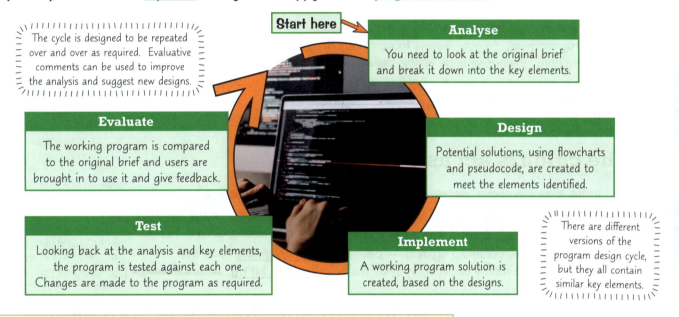

The cycle is designed to be repeated over and over as required. Evaluative comments can be used to improve the analysis and suggest new designs.

Start here

Analyse — You need to look at the original brief and break it down into the key elements.

Design — Potential solutions, using flowcharts and pseudocode, are created to meet the elements identified.

Implement — A working program solution is created, based on the designs.

Test — Looking back at the analysis and key elements, the program is tested against each one. Changes are made to the program as required.

Evaluate — The working program is compared to the original brief and users are brought in to use it and give feedback.

There are different versions of the program design cycle, but they all contain similar key elements.

Following the cycle with a simple program

EXAMPLE Briefly describe each stage of the program design cycle when used to create a currency converter.

Analyse	What conversion needs to take place? What types of data might be entered and need to be processed?
Design	A flowchart and pseudocode will be created.
Implement	A first version is written in Python, which allows for one value to be converted to another.
Test	Testing the program against the key elements of the original brief and fixing any errors that are found.
Evaluate	Potential users test the program and feedback is fed into the next version.

Q1 Suggest three things that potential users might consider when evaluating a program.

No need to check your tyre pressures before this cycle...

Using the program design cycle to break down the process of creating a program to solve a problem makes the whole process easier to deal with. It's all about working in a smart and efficient manner.

Section One — Introduction to Python

Section Two — Inputs, Outputs and Variables

Hello World!

Learning Objectives

It's finally time to crack on with some coding, starting with a classic task. Be sure to keep referring back to Section One as you go.

- Be able to use `print()` to output a message on the screen.
- Understand what a comment is and why they're used.

print() is used to output information on the user's screen

1) As you might have noticed from examples in Section One, `print()` is used to instruct the computer to output a message onto the screen. Here's how to use it:

   - In the Shell or Editor, write the word `print` and follow it with an opening bracket.
   - Next, write a message to be outputted within quote marks — one " at the start of the message, one " at the end.
   - Finish the line of code with a closing bracket.

   ```
   print("Hello World!")
   Hello World!
   ```

   In this example, `Hello World!` is being output to the user. As you're testing your own code, you're the user (for now).

2) The line of code won't do anything until you execute it. In programming, execute means to carry out the given instruction. Executing code is also called running code.

3) To execute the line, press the Return key (↵) if you are in the Shell, or save it and 'Run Module' if you are in the Editor (see pg.5 for a step-by-step guide on this).

 REAL WORLD CODE

All the text you see on a computer screen originated from a humble command like `print()`.

The colours act as a guide

In this book, you'll see the default colouring from IDLE.

1) In the example above, `print` is in purple and `Hello World!` is in green.
2) These colours aren't a part of Python itself — it's just the way the IDE displays them. There's no need to learn these colours or worry if you're seeing different ones.
3) A benefit of this colouring system — called syntax highlighting — is that syntax errors become easier to spot as the colours are a bit off.

```
Print("Hello World!")
print(Hello World!")
print"(Hello World!)"
```

Comments are used to help people understand code

EXAMPLE A comment is an annotation that a programmer leaves in their code to explain something about it. For example, a comment might explain what a particular line does.

Some code turns red when following a hash symbol — this is a comment. Anything on the line after the hash is part of the comment.

Comments can also go across multiple lines. To do this, you start and end it with triple quote marks (""").

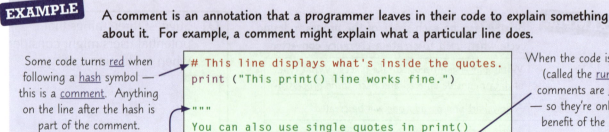

When the code is executed (called the runtime), comments are ignored — so they're only for the benefit of the reader.

Comments are also handy for leaving notes for your future self. You can also use a # to stop a line of code from running — useful if you don't want to delete it completely.

"World isn't available right now, please leave a comment..."

Once you've written your first line of code, you are officially a programmer — time to add Python to the old CV. Don't stop here though — you'll be able to get world to say 'hello' back later on in this section.

Variables

Learning Objectives

The next thing you need to know about are variables and how they allow you to keep track of values. I bet you're raring to get going now, so let's crack on with it!

- Understand what a variable is.
- Know the meaning of assignment and initialisation.
- To follow naming conventions.
- Be able to change the values of variables.

A variable holds a single value

1) A variable is a name that's used to represent a particular value held in the memory.
2) You can imagine them like a labelled box that can only hold one item at a time.
3) To assign a value to a variable in Python, you give it a name and use an equals sign.
4) The first time a variable is assigned a value, it's called initialisation.
5) Once a value has been assigned, the value is held and can be used by writing the variable's name.

`number = 496`

EXAMPLE Using variables to hold and then output some of my favourite things:

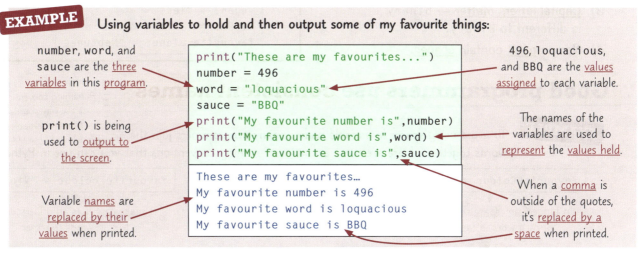

number, word, and sauce are the three variables in this program.

```
print("These are my favourites...")
number = 496
word = "loquacious"
sauce = "BBQ"
print("My favourite number is",number)
print("My favourite word is",word)
print("My favourite sauce is",sauce)
```

```
These are my favourites...
My favourite number is 496
My favourite word is loquacious
My favourite sauce is BBQ
```

496, loquacious, and BBQ are the values assigned to each variable.

print() is being used to output to the screen.

The names of the variables are used to represent the values held.

Variable names are replaced by their values when printed.

When a comma is outside of the quotes, it's replaced by a space when printed.

6) Not all values have quotation marks around them. Words need quotes around them to distinguish them from variable names (which have no quotation marks). Numbers are left without quotation marks so that you can perform maths operations — more on that in Section Three.

Assigning values to variables requires some care

It's important to correctly order your lines of code — doing it incorrectly will create errors in your program.

CODE ERRORS Here are a few common errors that happen when things get a bit mixed up.

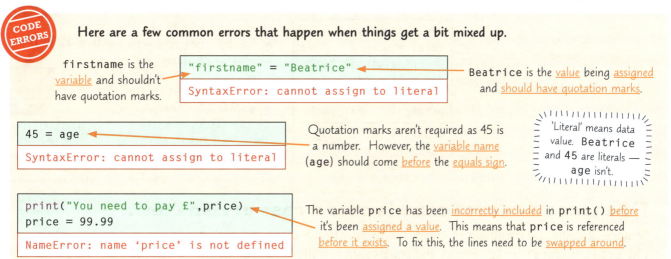

firstname is the variable and shouldn't have quotation marks.

```
"firstname" = "Beatrice"
SyntaxError: cannot assign to literal
```

Beatrice is the value being assigned and should have quotation marks.

```
45 = age
SyntaxError: cannot assign to literal
```

Quotation marks aren't required as 45 is a number. However, the variable name (age) should come before the equals sign.

'Literal' means data value. Beatrice and 45 are literals — age isn't.

```
print("You need to pay £",price)
price = 99.99
NameError: name 'price' is not defined
```

The variable price has been incorrectly included in print() before it's been assigned a value. This means that price is referenced before it exists. To fix this, the lines need to be swapped around.

Section Two — Inputs, Outputs and Variables

Variables

Variable names are set by programmers

1) The name given to a variable is for your convenience — the computer doesn't mind what you call them.
2) For example, to store a height, the following three snippets of code give the exact same output:

```
height = 180
print(height)
180
```

```
higt = 180
print(higt)
180
```

```
llanfairpwllgwyngyll = 180
print(llanfairpwllgwyngyll)
180
```

Readability is about how easily code can be understood.

3) Despite this freedom, our goal as good programmers is to make our code readable.
4) Misspelt or irrelevant variable names can confuse other people who read your code.

Golden rules to follow for variables names

1) A variable name can't start with a number.
2) You can't use symbols, except underscore (_).
3) Capital letters matter — `binary` is different to `Binary`.
4) Names can't contain spaces.

Q1 Cross out the invalid variable names below.

```
3rdPlace = "Jack"
BiNary = 0
vegan? = "Yes"
my_PAL = "Jill"
favourite planet = "Neptune"
```

Good programmers use consistent names

A naming convention is just the way you decide to name variables.

EXAMPLE To avoid using spaces in variable names, many programmers join the words together. Here are some examples of naming conventions that you can use in Python:

```
FavouriteColour = "Violet"
```
In UpperCamelCase the first letter of each word is capitalised.

```
favouriteColour = "Violet"
```
In lowerCamelCase, the first letter of every word after the first word is capitalised.

```
favourite_colour = "Violet"
```
Snake case uses an underscore to join words together.

As long as the names you use are consistent and meaningful, it doesn't matter what convention you choose to follow. In this book, we're going to use lowerCamelCase.

Variable values can vary

You can change the values of variables throughout your program by re-assigning them.

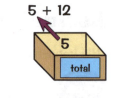

5 + 12

EXAMPLE Let's imagine you are measuring the total rainfall across a couple of days.

The variables are initialised here. Initialisation is the first assignment of a variable.

```
day = "Monday"
total = 5
print(day,total,"mm")
day = "Tuesday"
total = total + 12
print(day,total,"mm")

Monday 5 mm
Tuesday 17 mm
```

Suppose it rained 12 mm on Tuesday. The right-hand side of the equals sign is calculated first. So, the previous value of `total`, 5, is added to 12. The result, 17 (5 + 12), is assigned to the variable `total`, which overwrites the previous value.

The value of `day` has been changed, just by re-assigning it.

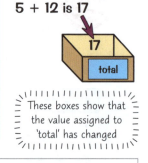

5 + 12 is 17

These boxes show that the value assigned to 'total' has changed

---

I'd choose a case of camels over a case of sssnakes...

Mathematicians and computer scientists are usually pretty close, but nothing causes friction between them like `total = total + 12`. For us, the equals sign just means assignment, not that both sides are equivalent.

Section Two — Inputs, Outputs and Variables

Practice Questions and Activities

Q1 Give two examples of `print()` that will lead to errors.

1 ....
2 ....

Q2 Describe what variables are and what they're used for.

....
....
....

Q3 For each of these scenarios, give a suitable example of a variable (or variables) and explain what they could be used for in the program.

Think about what information might need to be held and changed throughout the program.

a) A computer is linked to a sensor that is used to measure the height of a sunflower over the summer.

....
....

b) A video game that keeps track of the individual scores two players get in three separate levels, as well as their overall score.

....
....
....

Q4 For each program below, track the changes and circle what will be printed to the user's screen.

a)
```
netball = 5
tennis = 6
cricket = netball
netball = 6
tennis = 0
print(cricket)
```
0   5   6   Error

b)
```
football = "Twelve"
rugby = 5 + 2 + 2
12 = hockey
rugby = hockey + 1
squash = rugby - 1
print(squash)
```
9   12   13   Error

c)
```
swimming = 2
swimming = swimming + 4
dance = 2
dance = dance + 1
swimming = dance + swimming
print(swimming)
```
2   6   9   Error

Q5 Write a brief description of what is happening in each line of code and give the final output.

```
profit = 0
revenue = 10000
totalCosts = 4000
profit = revenue - totalCosts
print("The profit is",profit)
```

....
....
....

*Make sure to use the key words **initialisation** and **assignment**.*

....
....

Output: ....

Section Two — Inputs, Outputs and Variables

Getting User Inputs

Learning Objectives

So far, all the values of variables have been set by you. Variables become more useful when you're dealing with unknown values, like future user inputs.

- Understand what the input function does.
- To be able to assign user input to a variable.
- Use previous user inputs when printing.

print() is for outputting and input() is for inputting

1) When programmers want to show the user something on their screen, they use print().
2) When programmers want the user to give them something, they use the input function.
3) For now, think of a function as a command that performs a specific job. Functions will be covered in more detail in Section Seven.

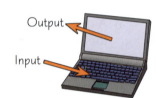

Think about how often you are asked to type something in when using a computer program. Each time this happens, the programmer will have used a function similar to input(). The difference is that usually it'll be used in a Graphical User Interface (GUI), whereas our programs, for now, use a Command Line Interface (CLI). Less exciting but the same principle.

input() is similar to print() but with a key difference

1) As both are functions, input() and print() work in a similar way.
2) You need to write the function name in lower case and then add opening and closing brackets.
3) Like print(), you don't actually need to put anything inside the brackets, but usually a message is written.

EXAMPLE There are two curious things about the example below.

Firstly, input() appears to work exactly like print(), because the message inside the brackets was printed to the screen.

```
input("Hello, how are you?")
print("Goodbye!")

Hello, how are you?
```

Secondly, Goodbye! won't appear straight away like you might expect. This is because the input function is waiting for you to type something in.

input() is giving the user a prompt to type something in

1) The message inside the input() brackets is also called the prompt.
2) It lets the user know that they should enter something.

EXAMPLE Here's the example above after the user has typed something in.

```
input("Hello, how are you?")
print("Goodbye!")

Hello, how are you?Terrible!
Goodbye!
```

The text in black is what the user has typed in.

3) After you type something in at the prompt, hit the Return (↵) key to signal that you're done.
4) Only then will the program carry on with its execution of the remaining lines of code.

Section Two — Inputs, Outputs and Variables

Getting User Inputs

Unless you use variables, user inputs are lost

1) Nobody likes to be ignored, but that's effectively what the code on the previous page did. The user typed in a <u>response</u>, and the <u>program didn't change</u> based on it.
2) When the user hits the <u>Return key</u>, the `input` <u>function</u> gives the program whatever the user typed in.
3) However, <u>unless</u> this is <u>held on to</u>, it's <u>immediately forgotten</u> about.

EXAMPLE Here's how to use `input()` with variables so that user responses can be held and used.

When the `input` function <u>returns</u> what the user <u>typed in</u>, it gets assigned to the variable `emotion`.

```
emotion = input("Hello, how are you? ")
print("Oh, you're feeling",emotion)
name = input("What's your name? ")
print(name,"I'm feeling good, not",emotion)
print("Goodbye!")
```

To make the prompt <u>neater</u>, a space is often left at the end. You can see this in the output below as there's a space before `Terrible!`.

At <u>runtime</u>, the outputs have been changed based on what was typed in.

```
Hello, how are you? Terrible!
Oh, you're feeling Terrible!
What's your name? Ivan
Ivan I'm feeling good, not Terrible!
Goodbye!
```

Whatever the user typed in previously will <u>replace</u> `emotion` in these `print` functions. The same goes for `name`.

Q1 Write additional lines of code to add in to the example above to ask three extra questions. For each one, print a suitable message back to the user that includes their response in some way.

Dealing with user input is full of uncertainty

1) The slight issue with the code example above, is that the user <u>could type anything</u> in, and it might not <u>fit with the code</u>.
2) To <u>adapt</u> the response (like giving a more sympathetic message back to poor Ivan), you'll need to wait for Section Four, which is when <u>selection</u> will be covered.
3) Users <u>can't</u> always <u>be trusted</u> either — Section Nine will help you deal with this.
4) The bottom line is that with `input()`, you <u>can't know</u> for sure what will be <u>typed in</u> until the program gets <u>executed</u> at runtime.

EXAMPLE Here's an example of what can go wrong if the user's answers don't fit the code.

```
Hello, how are you? What?
Oh, you're feeling What?
What's your name? None of your beeswax.
None of your beeswax. I'm feeling good, not What?
Goodbye!
```

Q2 Give the output of running the code below if the user first types in `Hello World` and then types in `41`.

```
number = 12
print("The number is",number)
number = input("Enter a number: ")
message = input("What is your message? ")
print(message, number)
```

Well I never...

Never trust a user to give a reasonable response...

Remember, the message inside the `input` function, the prompt, isn't the user input — it lets the user know what to do. So, whatever you write as a prompt isn't held in the variable, but what's typed at runtime is.

Section Two — Inputs, Outputs and Variables

Formatting Outputs

Learning Objectives

Formatting your outputs so they're neat and tidy is really important. This page has a few techniques which will help you do that.

- Be able to change the separator in `print()`.
- Understand what is meant by concatenation.
- Be able to escape characters.

You can use commas in print() but not input()

1) In `print()`, commas are used to separate text and variables. This is especially useful when you have multiple variables to output.

2) The default result for a comma, if outside of the quotes, is to be replaced with a space when shown to the user.

3) To change the separator from a space to something else, you can change the setting.

4) If you try to use a comma with `input()`, you'll get an error.

```
name = "Hans"
chosenLanguage = "Deutsch"
print(name,"is speaking",chosenLanguage)
```
```
Hans is speaking Deutsch
```

```
chosenLanguage = "Deutsch"
print("You are speaking",chosenLanguage,sep=": ")
```
```
You are speaking: Deutsch
```

```
name = "Hans"
place = input("Hi",name,"where are you from? ")
```
```
TypeError: input expected at most 1 argument, got 3
```

This comma doesn't get replaced by a colon and space as `sep` is a setting you're changing, not just another regular value.

A plus can also be used to add words (sort of)

1) When it's got numbers either side of it, the plus sign just does normal addition.

2) However, the plus sign is also used to join text. This is called concatenation.

3) You need text either side of the plus sign to do this — if one's a number and one's a word, you'll get an error.

4) Unlike the default separator in `print()`, the plus sign isn't replaced by a space.

5) Concatenation works in both `print()` and `input()`.

```
name = "Hans"
place = input("Hi " + name + ", where are you from? ")
print("Great, " + name + ". You're from " + place + ".")
```
```
Hi Hans, where are you from? Berlin
Great, Hans. You're from Berlin.
```

Backslashes are used to escape characters

1) Quotes are used to distinguish text from variable names. But what if you want to have quotes in the text?

2) To tell Python to ignore the normal use of the next character, add a backslash (\) before it.

3) This is known as an escape character, since without the backslash, Python would interpret it differently.

4) Other useful escape characters are `\n`, which makes the output go onto a new line, and `\t`, which adds a tab.

```
print("\"No way José!\",\n\tshe said.")
```
```
"No way José!",
    she said.
```

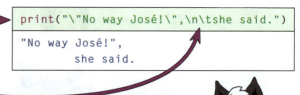

Concatenation — a country populated with feline super villains...

It's important to be able to format output exactly as you've been asked to. Unfortunately, this sometimes makes your prints and inputs a bit cluttered, with pluses, backslashes, and \ns all over the shop.

Section Two — Inputs, Outputs and Variables

Practice Questions and Activities

Q1 What is the purpose of the `input` function?

....

....

Q2 Why are variables used with the `input` function?

....

....

Q3 Give the outputs from these two programs, given the sequence of the inputs.

a) **Greg** is entered first, followed by **Carp**.

```
petName = input("What's your pet's name? ")
animal = input("What animal is " + petName + "? ")
print("You called your",animal,petName+"?!")
```

b) **5** is entered first, followed by **7**, and then **2**.

```
a = input()
b = input("2nd input: ")
c = 12
d = input("Enter a separator: ")
print(a,b,c,sep=d)
```

Q4 Write one `print()` line to produce the output shown.

```
"One", \Two
        "Three"
```

Q5 There are five errors in the program below. Circle these errors and rewrite the program without errors in the box below. Your new program should produce the intended output shown.

```
print("I am a sentient chatbot.")
1stName = Input(What's your name, BTW? ")
print("I'm sensing your name is.../n"+1stName)
```

Intended output:
```
I am a sentient chatbot.
What's your name, BTW? Sumaya
I'm sensing your name is...
Sumaya
```

Q6 Lea was taught to use the `input` function with nothing in the brackets. Give one advantage and one disadvantage of her using `input()` in this way.

```
print("Enter your age:")
age = input()
```

....

....

....

....

Section Two — Inputs, Outputs and Variables

Coding Challenges for Section Two

Right, it's time to put your Python knowledge to the test. Here are some challenges for you to tackle. Once you've had a go, visit the link on the contents page to download example Python programs for each challenge.

Challenge 1

An accountancy firm did a bit of snooping and found that lots of their employees have got into the habit of using weak passwords, such as "password123" or "ineedcoffee".

Make a program that asks an employee for their middle name, the name of their favourite type of pasta, any number of their choosing and a symbol character (e.g. & or £). Combine these into one password which can be shown to each employee as a suggestion for a stronger password option.

Challenge 2

It's 2.45 pm on a Friday afternoon and a History teacher senses that another test on the bubonic plague might go down badly. Code a version of the classroom memory game "I went to the market today" which can be played by the class instead. In the real-life version, the pupils take turns naming different items they might buy in alphabetical order as they move around the room. However, before saying their item, they must also say all of the items which were said before.

Your program should recreate this by doing the following:

- Start off by printing "I went to the market today and bought..."
- Then ask the first pupil to enter an item starting with the letter 'a'.
- Ask a second pupil to enter an item starting with the letter 'b' and continue this for the next few letters of the alphabet (for your sanity, you can stop when you've done the letter 'e').
- Between asking pupils, print "I went to the market today and bought" followed by all of the previous items entered.

Example output:

```
I went to the market and bought...
Enter an item starting with 'a': Apple
I went to the market today and bought an Apple.
Enter an item starting with 'b': Banana
I went to the market today and bought an Apple and a Banana.
```

To format the output appropriately, you can use the general rule that 'a' precedes a consonant, and 'an' precedes a vowel. This is fine here, but it doesn't always work — e.g. if your user buys an 'hourglass' this would display as 'a hourglass'.

Challenge 3

ASCII art is made just from the characters (letters, numbers and symbols) on a keyboard. As these can be easily copied and pasted, you'll often see these styles of artwork in web forums or in comments sections.

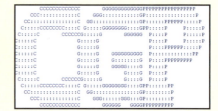

Using the print function, make a snake in the style of ASCII art (perhaps like the gorgeous specimen on the right). The user should also be asked to give a name for the snake which should be included somewhere in the output.

Before jumping straight into formatting in Python, it's probably worth making the ASCII art in a basic text editor like Notepad beforehand. You can then copy it in — but remember to add backslashes to escape characters where needed.

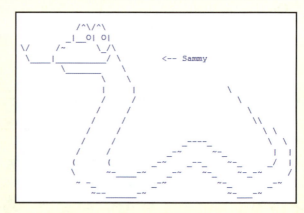

Section Three — Data Types and Operations

Data Types

Learning Objectives

It's time to take things up a notch and learn about data types and operations. This section will introduce you to programming techniques that'll take your coding to the next level.

- Learn about the need for data types.
- Learn about the most common data types.
- Understand the purpose of casting.
- Learn how to apply casting to data.

Data types categorise data

1) Data types tell the computer how to interpret the data it's given.
2) Each data type has its own processing rules — for example, arithmetic calculations can be carried out on integers but not on strings.

Identifying different types of data like numbers and letters is easy for humans, as is knowing what sort of things we can do with them. A computer can't know this unless there are defined data types.

There are various programming data types

Python uses the basic data types seen in the table below.

Data type	Description	Examples
Integer	A positive or negative whole number without a decimal point.	2001, -2010
String	A combination of letters, numbers and symbols in any order.	"Breakfast included", "04-05-77", "X, %, A, @"
Float	Any positive or negative number, including those with a decimal point.	15.10, -808.0
Boolean	Can only be represented by True or False and is case sensitive.	True/False

At first, all user inputs are normally treated as strings.

Floats are ideal for currency as most currencies require decimal points.

Q1 What are the most appropriate data types for the following?

Example	Data Type
-12.01	
"Leafy Lane"	
True	

Python will assign a data type

1) When creating variables, the most appropriate data type will be assigned automatically.
2) The most common data types you'll use in Python are integers and strings.
3) The type function will confirm the current data type.

EXAMPLE Here's an example of the type() command displaying the data type of three variables.

These quotation marks are required for strings.

```
a = "Pottery"
b = 19.77
c = False
print(type(a))
print(type(b))
print(type(c))
```

Each data type is displayed as an output.

```
<class 'str'>
<class 'float'>
<class 'bool'>
```

str and bool are shortened versions of string and Boolean.

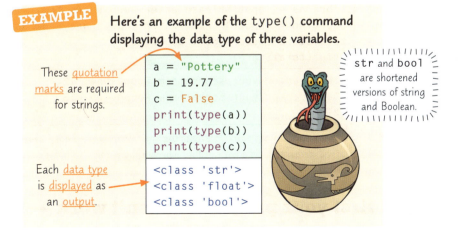

Data Types

Converting to a particular data type is called casting

1) Data may be need to be converted from one data type to another in order to do a calculation which only works on that data type.
2) Casting is important if, for example, data has been collected using the `input` function and then needs to be processed or used in a calculation.

EXAMPLE Here are examples of casting involving integers, strings and floats.

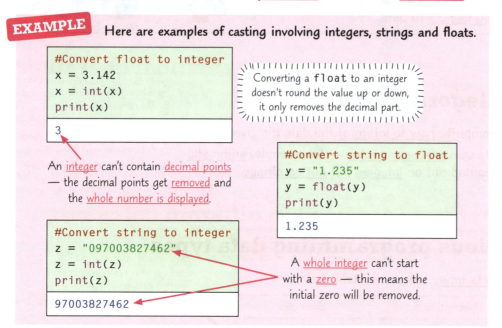

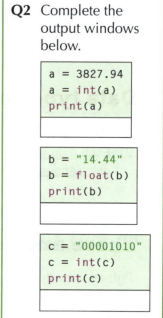

An integer can't contain decimal points — the decimal points get removed and the whole number is displayed.

Converting a `float` to an integer doesn't round the value up or down, it only removes the decimal part.

A whole integer can't start with a zero — this means the initial zero will be removed.

Q2 Complete the output windows below.

```
a = 3827.94
a = int(a)
print(a)
```

```
b = "14.44"
b = float(b)
print(b)
```

```
c = "00001010"
c = int(c)
print(c)
```

You can use casting to convert inputs from strings to numbers

In order to perform maths operations like addition, the data needs to be a number (integer or float).

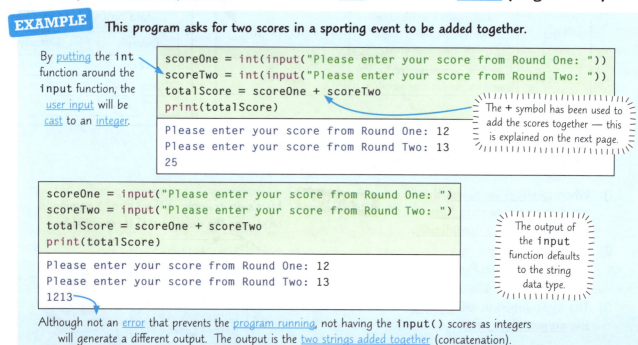

EXAMPLE This program asks for two scores in a sporting event to be added together.

By putting the `int` function around the `input` function, the user input will be cast to an integer.

The + symbol has been used to add the scores together — this is explained on the next page.

The output of the `input` function defaults to the string data type.

Although not an error that prevents the program running, not having the `input()` scores as integers will generate a different output. The output is the two strings added together (concatenation).

If at first your program doesn't work — call it version 1.0...

`int()` and `input()` are easily mixed up, so make sure you understand the difference before you move on. When using `int()` don't forget to close the brackets — it's an easy mistake to make that results in an error.

Section Three — Data Types and Operations

Arithmetic Operators

Learning Objectives

Computers are able to do calculations super quick. This is great because it means you can leave any sums in your code to them — no need to get that calculator out.

- Understand the need for arithmetic operators in Python.
- Learn about the most common arithmetic operators.
- Learn how to apply operators to carry out simple calculations.
- Learn how to use arithmetic operators in a larger program.

Arithmetic operators perform mathematical operations

1) Arithmetic operators are used to carry out mathematical calculations, e.g. addition, subtraction, multiplication and division.
2) Values need to be stored as numerical data types to be processed.

CODE ERRORS

```
a = 2 \ 2
print(a)
```
SyntaxError: unexpected character

A common error is using a backwards slash instead of a forward slash in a division.

Arithmetic operators are used in different calculations

This book uses the arithmetic operators in this table.

DIV is also called 'integer division' and 'quotient'.

Arithmetic operator	+	-	/	*	** (Exponentiation)	% (MOD)	// (DIV)
Description	Add	Subtract	Divide	Multiply	Raises to a power	Returns only the remainder after a division.	Returns the whole number part after a division.

EXAMPLE Here are some examples of how to carry out simple calculations.

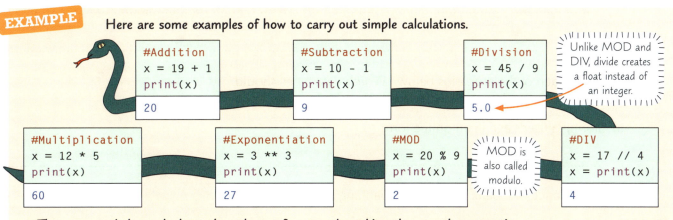

```
#Addition
x = 19 + 1
print(x)
```
20

```
#Subtraction
x = 10 - 1
print(x)
```
9

```
#Division
x = 45 / 9
print(x)
```
5.0

Unlike MOD and DIV, divide creates a float instead of an integer.

```
#Multiplication
x = 12 * 5
print(x)
```
60

```
#Exponentiation
x = 3 ** 3
print(x)
```
27

```
#MOD
x = 20 % 9
print(x)
```
2

MOD is also called modulo.

```
#DIV
x = 17 // 4
x = print(x)
```
4

The program below calculates the volume of a room by asking the user three questions.

```
height = int(input("How high is the room in metres?"))
width = int(input("How wide is the room in metres?"))
length = int(input("How long is the room in metres?"))
volume = height * width * length
print("The room is",volume,"square metres")
```

The three user input() values are multiplied together to calculate the volume.

```
How high is the room in metres?2
How wide is the room in metres?3
How long is the room in metres?3
The room is 18 square metres
```

The inputs must be cast to numbers as all user inputs are strings by default.

Q1 What would happen if you changed the type of the data from int to float in this room calculator example?

I've always found some arithmetic operators a bit divisive...

Using arithmetic operators to carry out simple calculations is a good way to hone your programming skills. Make sure you have a go at using casting to change the data type before you move on to the next page.

Section Three — Data Types and Operations

Practice Questions and Activities

Q1 Tick the correct data type for the values in the table.

Value	String	Boolean	Float
16.5			
Big Wednesday			
false			

Q2 Give a description of each of the following data types.

a) integer

....

b) string

....

c) float

....

Q3 The program shown uses casting.

```
a = 16.90
a = int(a)
print(a)
```

a) Give the output for the program.   Output ....

b) Describe the purpose of casting in Python.

....

....

Q4 Consider each of the scenarios below. Which data types should be assigned to the data used within each scenario?

a) Storing a user's age in an online form

....

b) The balance of a bank account in a banking app

....

c) Asking a user to describe the quality of their experience when using an online service

....

d) A True or False quiz program

....

Section Three — Data Types and Operations

Practice Questions and Activities

Q5 Describe the purpose of the program below and write in the final output.

```
number = int(input("Type in any whole number..."))
calcNumber = number * 3
calcNumber = calcNumber + 6
calcNumber = calcNumber / 3
guess = calcNumber - number
print("Doesn't matter what starting number you type, this answer is always...",guess)
```

....
....
....
....

Q6 There are three errors in the following program. Circle the errors in the code and describe them. Rewrite the program in the box below so that it runs correctly.

```
width = int(input("Enter width in metres: "))
height = input("Enter height in metres: "))
area = width x height
print("The area is",area "square metres.")
```

First error: ....

....

Second error: ....

....

Third error: ....

....

Q7 Complete the output box for each calculation.

a)
```
x = 1 + 99
print(x)
```

b)
```
x = 66 - 1
print(x)
```

c)
```
x = 81 / 9
print(x)
```

d)
```
x = 5 * 5
print(x)
```

e)
```
x = 10 % 6
print(x)
```

f)
```
x = 10 // 6
x = print(x)
```

Section Three — Data Types and Operations

Relational Operators

Learning Objectives
No, this isn't a page about navigating relationships. Instead, relational operators are all about comparing one thing to another thing.
- Understand the need for relational operators in Python.
- Learn about the most common relational operators.
- Learn about situations where relational operators can be used.
- Learn how to use relational operators in simple comparison programs.

Relational operators compare values

1) Relational operators are needed whenever you need to compare values (or expressions) within your program, e.g. comparing answers from two different users.
2) In Section Four, you'll see how these can be used within selection statements to make decisions.

There are a few relational operators to remember

1) You'll use the following six relational operators in Python.

Relational operator	==	!=	<	>	<=	>=
Description	Exactly equal to	Not equal to	Less than	Greater than	Less than or equal to	Greater than or equal to

2) Many systems require variables to be compared to each other, so there are lots of examples of their use in the real world.

- Central heating turning on or off when set to a specific temperature.
- Age restricted websites and applications allowing access if a user is over a certain age.
- Airport luggage scales letting you know if your suitcase is too heavy.
- Adaptive cruise control systems in cars accelerating or braking to maintain a constant speed.

A common error is using a single = sign, rather than the == required in a relational statement.

Have a think about which relational operators might be used in each of these systems.

Simple comparison programs use relational operators

EXAMPLE The example below uses relational operators to compare the heights of two people.

```
#greater than
zukoHeight = 120
hollyHeight = 110

print("Is Zuko taller than Holly?",zukoHeight > hollyHeight)
Is Zuko taller than Holly? True
```

These two variables are compared using the greater than operator.

Zuko is taller than Holly, so the comparison evaluates to True.

Relational operators — the love gurus of the programming world...

Relational operators are used in standard mathematics and are used in the same way here. But take care because there are some differences in the operators used, e.g. Python uses == instead of just =.

Section Three — Data Types and Operations

Boolean Operators

Learning Objectives

Yes or no, true or false, on or off, computers love binary choices. In order to make these binary choices, you need to know how to use Boolean operators.

- Understand how Boolean logic is similar to binary data and logic gates.
- Learn about the Boolean truth tables.
- Learn about situations where Boolean operators can be used.
- Learn how to use Boolean operators in simple programs.

Boolean operators work with the Boolean data type

1) The CPU of a computer (which is the device actually executing your Python code) is made up of billions of parts that work like switches.
2) A switch can be either on or off. That's one of the reasons why binary is used in computing — switches are a simple way to represent binary with on being '1' and off being '0'.
3) Boolean logic is a simple way to represent problems. It also fits really well with computing, since `True` can represent '1' and `False` can represent '0'.
4) The switches in hardware (when carefully arranged into circuits called logic gates) can be used to implement Boolean logic that uses Boolean and relational operators.
5) The three basic Boolean operators are `not`, `and` and `or` — they only work with Boolean values.
6) Their operation can be expressed in truth tables, which show all of the possible combinations of a Boolean operator. 0/False and 1/True can be used interchangeably.

Boolean operators can also be called logical operators

not	
Input	Output
0	1
1	0

The output is always the opposite value of the input.

and		
Input A	Input B	Output
0	0	0
0	1	0
1	0	0
1	1	1

If both inputs are 1, the output is 1. Otherwise the output is 0.

or		
Input A	Input B	Output
0	0	0
0	1	1
1	0	1
1	1	1

If one or both inputs are 1, the output is 1. Otherwise the output is 0.

Boolean operators always evaluate to True or False

EXAMPLE Here are some examples of Boolean operators in action.

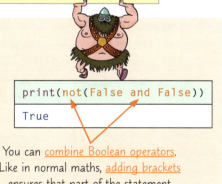

```
print(True or False)
True
```

Evaluating a statement is finding its result — here it's `True`, as row three of the `or` truth table above shows.

```
print(not 1)
False
```

You can use `True` and `False` interchangeably with 1 and 0. Using other values can lead to weird and incorrect results, so stick to only Booleans.

```
print("F" and "T")
'T'
```

```
print(not(False and False))
True
```

You can combine Boolean operators. Like in normal maths, adding brackets ensures that part of the statement is evaluated first. Statements that evaluate to Boolean values are also called Boolean expressions.

Section Three — Data Types and Operations

Boolean Operators

and, or and not let you create Boolean expressions

1) **and**, **or** and **not** can be used to create complex Boolean expressions.
2) **and** and **or** allow you to check two Boolean expressions in a single expression.

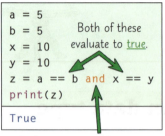

Both sets of variables must match, which they do.

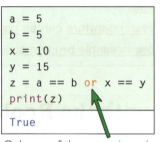

Only one of the comparisons is True, meeting the or criteria

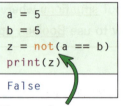

The use of not reverses the output that would otherwise be True.

Notice that **and**, **or** and **not** are in lowercase. Brackets are also used in the **not** example as it's being applied to the statement a == b.

Relational operators are useful in Boolean expressions

EXAMPLE Relational operators like < and > (see p.26) can be also combined with Boolean operators to create more complex comparisons. Here are a few examples that use different relational operators.

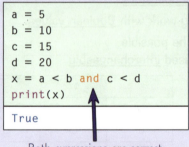

Both expressions are correct; therefore the result is True.

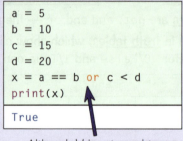

Although 'a' is not equal to 'b', 'c' is smaller than 'd' so the or statement is still True.

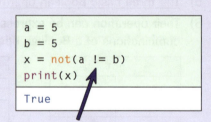

A double negative — the expression is False, but the not operator inverts it to True.

and can be used for a simple number checker

EXAMPLE Imagine playing a lottery-style game where only two numbers are drawn. The only chance of winning is if both numbers drawn match your own.

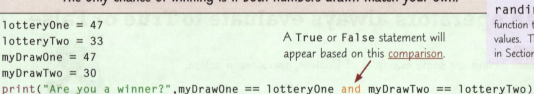

A True or False statement will appear based on this comparison.

Lottery-based programs can use the **randint** function to generate values. This is covered in Section Seven.

Q1 Give the output for the simple lottery game above.

Boolean operators — selling diet plans to a ghost near you...

You've now been introduced to three different types of operator — arithmetic, relational and Boolean. Have a go at scribbling down a quick definition for each one and then flick back to check if you got them right.

Section Three — Data Types and Operations

String Handling

Learning Objectives

Strings can be handled in a variety of ways. They can be made of a combination of letters, numbers and symbols that appear in any order.

- Understand the meaning of the term string handling.
- Learn how to change strings to upper or lower case.
- Learn about counting characters in strings and string slicing.
- Learn about character codes and how to use the functions chr() and ord().

String handling is using tools to process strings

1) Unlike numbers or True and False statements (Boolean), strings are more difficult to process.
2) Strings are always created as a response to the input function — e.g. "How do you feel?"

Changing the case of a string

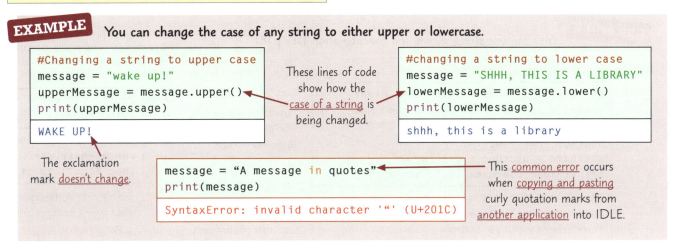

EXAMPLE You can change the case of any string to either upper or lowercase.

```
#Changing a string to upper case
message = "wake up!"
upperMessage = message.upper()
print(upperMessage)
```
```
WAKE UP!
```

These lines of code show how the case of a string is being changed.

```
#changing a string to lower case
message = "SHHH, THIS IS A LIBRARY"
lowerMessage = message.lower()
print(lowerMessage)
```
```
shhh, this is a library
```

The exclamation mark doesn't change.

```
message = "A message in quotes"
print(message)
```
```
SyntaxError: invalid character '"' (U+201C)
```

This common error occurs when copying and pasting curly quotation marks from another application into IDLE.

Counting the number of characters in a string

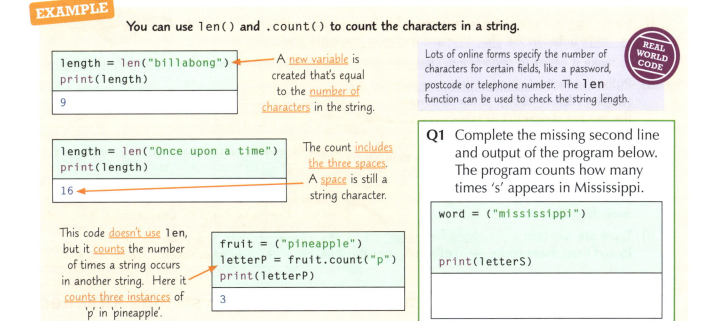

EXAMPLE You can use len() and .count() to count the characters in a string.

```
length = len("billabong")
print(length)
```
```
9
```

A new variable is created that's equal to the number of characters in the string.

Lots of online forms specify the number of characters for certain fields, like a password, postcode or telephone number. The len function can be used to check the string length.

REAL WORLD CODE

```
length = len("Once upon a time")
print(length)
```
```
16
```

The count includes the three spaces. A space is still a string character.

Q1 Complete the missing second line and output of the program below. The program counts how many times 's' appears in Mississippi.

```
word = ("mississippi")


print(letterS)
```

This code doesn't use len, but it counts the number of times a string occurs in another string. Here it counts three instances of 'p' in 'pineapple'.

```
fruit = ("pineapple")
letterP = fruit.count("p")
print(letterP)
```
```
3
```

Section Three — Data Types and Operations

String Handling

An index lets you specify a position in a string

1) Python automatically assigns a numerical value to each character's position in a string.
2) Look at the index table below for the string 'white rabbit'.

String	w	h	i	t	e		r	a	b	b	i	t
Positive index	0	1	2	3	4	5	6	7	8	9	10	11
Negative index	-12	-11	-10	-9	-8	-7	-6	-5	-4	-3	-2	-1

Positive indexing starts at the beginning of a string and negative indexing starts at the end.

3) You can use indices to slice strings, giving you a substring or single character.

```
#1 (one letter)
string = "white rabbit"
print(string[-5])

a
```

Using a single index value that isn't followed by a colon allows you to output a single letter.

```
#2 (first three letters)
string = "white rabbit"
print(string[0:3])

whi
```

string[a:b] creates a substring from position 'a' to position 'b - 1'. So [0:3] gives whi, rather than whit.

```
#3 (10th letter onwards)
string = "white rabbit"
print(string[9:])

bit
```

[9:] starts at index 9 and, when 'b' isn't provided, carries on to the end.

EXAMPLE
You can use string slicing and concatenation (see p.18) to create a username.

It's important to consider whether any spaces or punctuation will be needed in a concatenated string.

```
first = input("Enter your first name: ")
second = input("Enter your second name: ")
userOne = first[0:2]
userTwo = second[0:3]
userName = userOne + userTwo
print("Your username is:",userName)
```
```
Enter your first name: Isobel
Enter your second name: Grace
Your username is: IsGra
```

This comma is used to separate the printed quote from the variable.

Don't forget, the first character when slicing strings is at index position zero.

```
four = "2" + 2
print(four)

TypeError: can only
concatenate str
(not "int") to str
```

This error is displayed when trying to concatenate a string and an integer in the same statement.

Each character has a numerical code

1) Each character in a string is represented in binary using a character set that converts between the character and a unique character code.
2) To make it easier to understand, character codes are usually expressed as a denary/decimal number.
3) Python uses the Unicode® character set (which includes ASCII). Examples from this set are shown in this table.

Character	%	&	1	2	A	B	Y	Z	a	z
Code	37	38	49	50	65	66	89	90	97	122

4) The codes in ASCII/Unicode® are sequential, meaning the code for 'H' is one more than 'G'.
5) The codes explain why something like "%" < "&" is True and why something like "A" > "a" is False.
6) There are two built-in functions for converting to and from these codes — ord() and chr().

```
# chr() converts the code to its character
print("The character for the code 33 is",chr(33))

# ord() converts the character to its code
print("The code for the character C is",ord("C"))

The character for the code 33 is !
The code for the character C is 67
```

I'm selling my computer at a great price — no strings attached...

You might've spotted that the positive index always starts with a value of '0', but in the negative index, it starts from -1. Indexing can be tricky so make sure you work through all the examples on these pages.

Section Three — Data Types and Operations

Practice Questions and Activities

Q1 Describe two scenarios where a relational operator would be useful.

1 ....

2 ....

Q2 Describe the meaning of the following relational operators.

a) <= ....

b) != ....

c) == ....

Q3 Complete the output for the following train speed control program.

```
currentSpeed = 85
targetSpeed = 90
print("Target speed exceeded: ",currentSpeed > targetSpeed)
```

Q4 For each question below write a line of code that can be typed directly into the Shell that will provide a True or False response.

a) Is 250 greater than 240?

b) Is 1000 exactly equal to 1000?

c) Is 1999 not equal to 1999?

Q5 State the names of three different string handling techniques.

1 ....

2 ....

3 ....

Section Three — Data Types and Operations

Practice Questions and Activities

Q6 Use the string in the table to fill in the outputs below.

String	T	e	a		f	o	r		f	o	u	r
Positive index	0	1	2	3	4	5	6	7	8	9	10	11
Negative index	-12	-11	-10	-9	-8	-7	-6	-5	-4	-3	-2	-1

a) `print(string[0:3])`

b) `print(string[4:])`

c) `print(string[-8:-5])`

Q7 There are three errors in the program below. Identify and describe these errors on the lines below. Then rewrite the program so that it runs correctly and gives the output "Underground".

```
a = "Under
b = "ground"
c =(a - b)
print(a)
```

Corrected program:

```
Underground
```

First error: ....

Second error: ....

Third error: ....

Q8 The program shown on the right is the username creation program shown on p.30.

In the code box below, write a new version of this program that asks the user for their year of birth. This value should be added to the end of the username.

Give the output if the name Devveena Thulsie and the year 1984 were entered.

```
01  first = input("Enter your first name: ")
02  second = input("Enter your second name: ")
03  userOne = first[0:2]
04  userTwo = second[0:3]
05  userName = userOne + userTwo
06  print("Your username is:",userName)
```

Q9 Give the name of two computer character sets.

....

Q10 Give two functions that can be used to convert any character to Unicode and back again. Describe what each function does.

....

....

Coding Challenges for Section Three

Make yourself a drink and grab a biscuit before sitting down to tackle the coding exercises below. Once you've had a go, visit the link on the contents page to download the example Python programs for each challenge.

Challenge 1

The diagram shows the flight path of a satellite around the earth.

A program is needed to calculate the distance between points A and B shown on the diagram. The program should assume that the flight path is circular and points A and B are the same distance apart in both directions along the flight path.

The program should do the following:
- ask the user for the straight-line distance in miles between points A and B
- convert the value to kilometres
- calculate the distance from point A to point B along the flight path
- output the distance (to the nearest kilometre) to the user

Hint: to work out the distance from A to B along the flight path you'll need to work out the circumference of the entire circular flight path. The formula for calculating the circumference of a circle is diameter × pi.

In your program use a value of 3.142 for pi and assume that 1 mile is equal to 1.6 kilometres.

See p.74 for how to use a more accurate value of pi from the `math` module — there's an example program to download which shows this in action.

Challenge 2

A group of students have asked you to create a pocket money savings calculator. They'd like a way to see how much money they can save in a year if they don't spend all of their pocket money each week.

The program should do the following:
- ask the user how much pocket money they get per week
- ask how much of their money they normally spend each week
- use the remaining amount to calculate a total for the year

Remember that amounts of money usually have two decimal places.

Challenge 3

You've been asked to create a simple game for children to help them learn the spelling of an animal name.

The program should store an animal name, e.g. 'elephant', and then provide the first and last letters, and total number of letters, as clues. The user then gets one try to guess the animal. The program should respond `True` or `False`, depending on their answer.

Challenge 4

You've been asked by a languages teacher to create a mini game that asks students to come up with a word that has a certain number of letters.

The program should:
- prompt the user for a 7-letter word
- respond with a statement and followed by `True` or `False` if their word has the correct number of letters
- repeat the process for a 4-letter word

Section Three — Data Types and Operations

Section Four — Selection

if Statements

Learning Objectives

So far, your programs have only followed a straight path. Programming, like life, is a tiny bit more complex. It's time to make some decisions...

- Understand the purpose of selection blocks.
- Know the syntax of an if statement.
- Execute code based on a condition.

Selection blocks are all about making decisions

1) Proper programs are made from combinations of three building blocks — sequence, selection, and iteration.
2) Sequence covers what's done in the book so far — all of the lines are executed one-by-one from top to bottom until the program ends. This means that the flow of the program is always the same.
3) A group of selection statements (also known as a selection block) gives programmers control over the flow of their code.
4) Iteration also gives flow control, but that'll be covered in more detail in Section Five.

A block is a section of related code.

if is needed in order to carry out selection

1) The if statement is Python's way of performing selection.
2) You might follow a similar structure to an if statement in real life — e.g. "if today is Friday, then I'll treat myself to a pizza".
3) "today is Friday" is a Boolean condition — it's either True or False.
4) The result (tucking into a pizza) only happens if the condition is True.

See p.27-28 for more on Boolean operators.

EXAMPLE Let the user know it's time for pizza only if it's Friday.

The statement begins with a lowercase if, followed by the Boolean condition after the space.

This is the code that executes only if the condition is True. It's part of the if block because it's indented.

```
day = input("What day is it? ")

if day == "Friday":
    print("It's pizza time!")

print("Have a good day!")
```

```
What day is it? Friday
It's pizza time!
Have a good day!
```

This colon is essential. It indicates that you've finished writing the condition.

Remember, == is testing whether the left hand side is equal to the right hand side.

Q1 What happens if friday is entered as input?

....

....

Q2 Modify the code so that it's pizza time every day except Friday.

Indents are an important part of syntax

1) An indent is a gap at the start of a line of code. This might not seem like much but they have a really important role.
2) In the pizza time example above, you can see an indent at the start of the line after the colon.
3) Without this indent, Python doesn't know what is and what isn't a result of that decision — `print("It's pizza time!")` is, but `print("Have a good day!")` isn't.

It's important to make sure every line inside the if block has the same indentation.

Q3 Adapt the code so that the user can set pizza day to be some other day of the week.

Q4 Following the decision that it's pizza time, ask the user for three toppings, and print these out as a summary afterwards. This should only happen if day is given as Friday.

Use the Tab key to create your indentations for these questions.

if Statements

Diamonds are for selection

EXAMPLE Flowcharts are really good for visualising program flow. This example shows the pizza time program from the previous page.

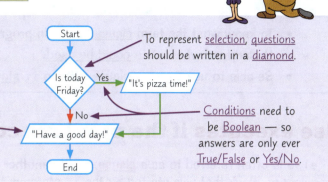

To represent selection, questions should be written in a diamond.

Conditions need to be Boolean — so answers are only ever True/False or Yes/No.

Since print("Have a good day!") is outside the if block, it gets executed regardless of the selection that came before.

The syntax rules for selection are strict

1) There are a few really common mistakes that are made when working with selection.

CODE ERRORS Each of the code examples below have a single error. If you want to test yourself, cover the text below each error and see if you can work out what went wrong.

```
age=72
if age>=65 or<18:
    print ("Free bus pass.")
Invalid Syntax
```
The condition hasn't been fully written out. Both sides of or need to be an expression — if age>=65 or age<18:

```
age = 72
if age >= 65:
print("Free bus pass.")
Invalid Syntax
```
The code in the if block hasn't been indented. Click at the start of the print line and hit 'Tab' to add it.

```
age= 72
if age >= 65
    print("Free bus pass.")
Invalid Syntax
```
A colon is missing after the condition.

2) Many IDEs will automatically add a Tab-sized indent after the colon is added and Enter is pressed.
3) The size of the indent is up to the programmer. Any size indent is okay, but the size must be the same in each block — e.g. the lines of code indented inside an if block.
4) Apart from indents, Python is pretty relaxed about white space. Including white space in your code can make it easier to read and it won't cause errors. For example, in the code examples above, the amount of white space between and within the lines of code varies, but this isn't the cause of the errors.

White space is any gap in code — like an empty line, an indent or a space.

Boolean operators can be added to conditions

1) Operators can be used to create Boolean expressions (for a reminder see p.27-28) — the example here shows some in action.

2) As long as the overall expression only evaluates to True or False, it can be used as a condition in selection.

```
age = int(input("What's your age? "))
testPass = input("Have you passed the test? ")

if age > 16 and (testPass == "Yes" or testPass == "Y"):
    print("Well done - you can drive.")
```
```
What's your age? 17
Have you passed the test? Y
Well done - you can drive.
```

This condition really has three mini expressions in it — each one is Boolean.

---

if stillUpToTheChallenge == True and patience != "wearing thin":

Getting into the habit of only using the Tab key for indentations is a great way of making sure the size of your indentations is consistent. There's no universal size of Tab, but in your IDE it'll stay the same.

Section Four — Selection

else Clause

Learning Objectives

`if` is really useful, but when used on its own, the decisions really only have one possible outcome. Using `else` gives you an alternative option.

- To know what the term clause means in programming.
- Understand when `else` could be used.
- Be able to use an `else` clause with an `if` statement.

else executes if the previous conditions were false

1) `else` is often referred to as a clause, as it's another part of the selection block that was started by the `if` statement.
2) A clause is code that can't work on its own but is useful when combined with other code. `if` isn't a clause as it'll work perfectly fine on its own.
3) The `else` clause is an optional part of an `if` statement — it doesn't work on its own.
4) The purpose of `else` is to provide an option when the previous conditions are False. This is why it doesn't have its own condition — it works as a catch-all.

You can also use the `else` clause in `for` and `while` statements.

EXAMPLE Write a program that will take a percentage as input and check to see if a student has passed or failed a test. Set 40% to be the minimum percentage for a pass.

```
percent = float(input("Enter the percentage: "))

if percent >= 40 and percent <= 100:
    print("Test pass.")
else:
    print("Test fail. Sorry about that.")

print("Goodbye.")
```

```
Enter the percentage: 39
Test fail. Sorry about that.
Goodbye.
```

Percentages can be decimals, so the input is cast to be a float, not just an int.

Remember that indents should be consistent — both for the start of the statements and the code inside (called the 'body').

The `if` statement is checked first — if the input was between 40 and 100 (inclusive), it would've printed "Test pass."...

...but, as 39 was inputted, the condition is False and the code inside `else` gets executed instead.

Q1 Modify the code above to display how many percentage points above or below the pass/fail threshold the student was.

Code outside selection blocks isn't part of the decision

1) To recap, the code inside the `if` statement only gets executed if the condition is True. However, if it's False, the code inside the `if` statement gets ignored and the execution continues. If there's an `else` clause (see the example above) the code inside it will be executed instead.
2) Code outside of the selection, like `print("Goodbye")`, is executed regardless of what happens in the selection block.

If you liked the `else` clause, then you'll love the santa clause...

If you're using an `else` clause, make sure that it comes at the end of the `if` statement — like six-year-old me lost in the supermarket, `else` really doesn't like being alone. And don't forget about those indents.

Section Four — Selection

elif Clause

Learning Objectives

A selection block with `if` and `else` gives two options — something happens, or it doesn't. It's often simpler to consider many options at once — that's where the `elif` clause comes in.

- Be able to use an `elif` clause with an `if` statement.
- Understand when and when not to use `elif` with `if` and `else`.
- Be able to nest selection blocks within other selection blocks.

More conditions can be added using the elif clause

1) `elif` clauses can be built into selection blocks.
2) When these clauses are used, they always sit after `if` and before `else`.
3) The purpose of `elif` is to give the program another condition to check for in a situation where the previous condition was False.
4) You can have multiple `elif` clauses in one selection block, but only one `if` statement and one `else` clause.

elif is a made-up Python keyword — a combination of else and if, which is handy for remembering where it's used.

EXAMPLE

Adapt the program from the previous page for the GCSE 9-1 grading system. Take 90% or more to be a grade 9, all the way down to 10% or more being a grade 1 — for the grades in between, e.g. a grade 8 would be given to a percentage of 80% or more that's less than 90%.

```
percent = float(input("Enter the percentage: "))
if percent >= 90:
    print("Grade 9")
elif percent >= 80:
    print("Grade 8")
elif percent >= 70:
    print("Grade 7")
elif percent >= 60:
    print("Grade 6")
elif percent >= 50:
    print("Grade 5")
elif percent >= 40:
    print("Grade 4")
elif percent >= 30:
    print("Grade 3")
elif percent >= 20:
    print("Grade 2")
elif percent >= 10:
    print("Grade 1")
else:
    print("Test fail. Sorry.")
print("Goodbye.")
```

if always starts the selection off. Make sure this condition is the first one that you want checked.

elif is used in the same way as if, but it has a condition that's only checked if the preceding condition was False.

else can be used at the end of the selection block for anything not covered by the previous conditions.

If percent is greater than or equal to 90, Grade 9 gets printed, and the rest of the selection block gets skipped.

```
Enter the percentage: 92.5
Grade 9
Goodbye.
```

If the percentage entered was 62, the conditions are checked one-by-one, until one condition is True. Then the rest of the selection block is skipped.

```
Enter the percentage: 62
Grade 6
Goodbye.
```

If 5.2 was entered, then none of the conditions in the selection block are True. This means the code in the else clause is executed.

```
Enter the percentage: 5.2
Test fail. Sorry.
Goodbye.
```

Q1 Give the output of the example code above when...
  a) 101.9 is entered.
  b) 'Sixty' is entered.

Q2 Modify the example code above to ensure that only percentages entered that range from 0 to 100 will be graded.

Q3 When the grades follow a uniform pattern like they do in the example above, you can calculate the grades without using selection at all. Write an alternative solution that does this.

Section Four — Selection

elif Clause

Be careful of using multiple ifs in place of elifs

1) The code on the previous page could've been written using multiple if statements.
2) For some inputs, this would work exactly the same as before, e.g. if the percentage entered is 15.

```
Enter the percentage: 15
Grade 1
Goodbye.
```

3) However, for bigger percentages, it leads to a logic error as it doesn't work as expected.

```
Enter the percentage: 47
Grade 4
Grade 3
Grade 2
Grade 1
Goodbye.
```

```
percent = float(input("Enter the percentage: "))

if percent >= 90:
    print("Grade 9")
if percent >= 80:
    print("Grade 8")
if percent >= 70:
    print("Grade 7")
# Code for Grades 6 - 2 is hidden.
if percent >= 10:
    print("Grade 1")
else:
    print("Test fail. Sorry.")

print("Goodbye.")
```

This comment shows that the code for Grades 6 - 2 are still part of the program but have been hidden from view.

Exam grading is an example of a mutually exclusive problem — one where you can't have multiple outcomes occurring at once, like getting multiple grades for one exam.

4) This happens because each if statement is starting a new selection block, so every condition is checked as the code runs.
5) To fix this example, each condition could be modified to check for the complete range.

```
if percent >= 80 and percent < 90:
    print("Grade 8")
```

6) However, using elifs is still more efficient. Every if statement has to be checked by the program, which is a waste of time if a condition has already been evaluated to True.

Code is efficient when it doesn't waste time or use memory unnecessarily.

7) elif and else clauses are only checked if the previous conditions in that block were False. If one of the previous conditions was True, then the following clauses are ignored as it's unnecessary to check them.

Embedding code blocks within others is called nesting

EXAMPLE Write a program for a theme park that checks a visitor's height and age to see if they're allowed to ride a rollercoaster. The maximum height allowed is 200 cm and the minimum age is 13.

This selection block is nested within the outer selection block — the additional level of indentation shows this.

This else belongs to the outer selection block.

```
age = int(input("How old are you? "))

if age >= 13:
    height = float(input("What is your height? "))
    if height <= 200:
        print("Enjoy the rollercoaster.")
    else:
        print("Unfortunately, you are too tall to ride.")
else:
    print("Unfortunately, you are too young to ride.")

How old are you? 12
Unfortunately, you are too young to ride.
```

This is an example of where elif isn't really suitable since being 13 and over 2 metres tall is possible.

This problem could be solved in a similar way just by using a longer condition with Boolean and. The benefit of nesting instead is that you only need to ask for their height if their age is 13 or above.

What would you get if if and else had a baby? That's right, ilsf...

Nesting will become necessary to solve lots of the problems later in this book. You've heard this before, but keep those indents consistent when doing this — otherwise your nest will be full of unwanted errors.

Practice Questions and Activities

Q1 a) What are selection blocks used for in programming?

....

....

b) Name the type of statement that is used for selection in Python.

....

Q2 The code below is from a program that places people in a particular generation based on their birth year. The code uses two of the three basic building blocks of programming — sequence and selection.

```
01  name = input("What is your name? ")
02  birthYear = int(input("What year were you born in? "))
03
04  if birthYear >= 2012:
05      print(name+", you are a member of Generation Alpha.")
```

> There are line numbers in this program but they don't affect the code. You can show these numbers in IDLE by selecting Show Line Numbers in the Options menu.

a) What would be shown to the user if `Fatima` and then `2004` were entered?

....

b) Inputting `Johann` and then `2k13` would result in an error. Which line would cause the error and why?

....

....

c) State the line numbers that show sequence and explain why.

....

....

d) State the line numbers which show selection and explain why.

....

....

e) The program at the start of the question is continued below. Fill in the gaps so that more generations can be classified. Use the table to define the ranges.

```
06  _____ birthYear ____ _____
07      print(name+", you are a member of _____.")
08  _____ birthYear ____ _____
09      print(name+", you are a Millennial.")
10  _____
11      print("Mmm, I'm not sure what to classify you as...")
```

Generation	Time span
Millennial Generation	1981-1995
Generation Z	1995-2012
Generation Alpha	After 2012

f) Describe the flow of execution that occurs from line 4 onwards when the `birthYear` is 1982.

....

....

....

....

....

Section Four — Selection

Practice Questions and Activities

Q3 Work through these programs to determine how many times `Hi` will be outputted to the user.

a)
```
01   animal = "Cat"
02   if animal == "Cat":
03       print("Hi")
04   elif animal == "Cat":
05       print("Hi")
06   elif animal == "Mouse":
07       print("Hi")
08   else:
09       print("Hi")
```

How many times is `Hi` printed? ....

Reasoning: ....

....

....

b)
```
01   animal = "Cat"
02   if animal == "Cat":
03       print("Hi")
04   if animal == "Cat":
05       print("Hi")
06   if animal == "Mouse":
07       print("Hi")
08   else:
09       print("Hi")
```

How many times is `Hi` printed? ....

Reasoning: ....

....

....

Q4 This code is for the beginning of a video game. An error is preventing it from working properly.

a) What type of error is this?

....

b) One line causes the error in the program. Explain why and rewrite this line to fix it.

```
01   ready = input("Are you ready to begin? ")
02   if ready == "Yes" or "Y" or "y":
03       print("Let's get started!")
04   else:
05       print("Oh! I see...")
```

```
Are you ready to begin? Absolutely not.
Let's get started!
```

....

....

....

Q5 This program uses nested selection to check if three people have got the same date of birth. Rewrite the code from line 5 onwards so that selection is used, but without nesting.

```
01   person1 = input("What is person 1's birthday? ")
02   person2 = input("What is person 2's birthday? ")
03   person3 = input("What is person 3's birthday? ")
04
05   if person1 == person2:
06     if person2 == person3:
07       print("Wow, what are the odds?")
08     else:
09       print("They aren't all the same.")
10   else:
11     print("They aren't all the same.")
```

```
What is person 1's birthday? 29/06/2000
What is person 2's birthday? 06/06/2009
What is person 3's birthday? 02/11/2001
They aren't all the same.
```

Section Four — Selection

Coding Challenges for Section Four

It's time to put the knowledge you've gained to the test. Don't rush through the questions — good programming takes time. Have a crack at the challenges below before visiting the link on the contents page for the Python files.

Challenge 1

Sara is planning her revision timetable for her exams. The table below shows how Sara breaks up her week.

	Monday	Tuesday	Wednesday	Thursday	Friday
Morning	Computer Science	Maths		Computer Science	Music
Afternoon		Science	English	Computer Science	

Write a program for Sara that:
- Asks what day it is and then ask for the time in the 24-hour clock format, e.g. 17.32.
- Tells Sara what subject she should be revising at that point in time, if any.
- Gives her a specific topic to study for two sessions of Computer Science all day Thursday (lucky Sara).

Challenge 2

A Manchester-based airline is having a 'Super Summer Sale'. All flights above 1000 miles have a discount applied to the normal ticket price — 15% for standard class and 30% for first class. Flights that are 1000 miles or less have a 7.5% discount applied to standard-class tickets and a 10% discount applied to first-class tickets.

Your program should meet the following requirements:
- A customer is asked to enter one of the four destinations below and the type of ticket. They then receive the correct discounted price.
- Alternatively, if a customer is flying to a destination not in the table, then they should be able to enter the normal ticket price, the ticket type, and the flight distance before receiving the correct discounted price.
- All prices printed to the customer should be given in pounds and pence, e.g. £220.55.

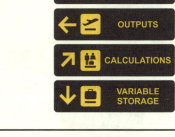

Destination	Normal ticket price (£)		Flight distance (miles)
	Standard class	First class	
Ålesund Vigra (AES)	106	N/A	700
Shanghai Hongqiao (SHA)	1000	2200	5700
Bucharest Otopeni (OTP)	95	190	1400
Toulouse (TLS)	115	210	690

round() is a useful function for displaying prices.

```
print(round(35.986,2))
35.99
```

Set this number to the number of decimal places you want to round to.

Challenge 3

A website requires users to set a password. Predictably, users keep setting rubbish ones that are easy to guess. You've been asked to write a program to help stop this happening.

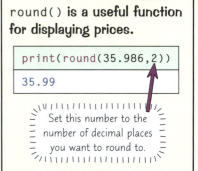

A useful tool to use here is isdigit(). E.g. "H".isdigit() would return False, as H isn't a number.

Your program should:
- Ask the user for a password, but if it has fewer than 8 characters or has a number as the first character, reject it and give them one yourself (it doesn't matter what this is — you could integrate your code from Challenge 1 on p.20 for this).
- After the password has been entered, ask the user to re-enter the password (either their accepted password or the generated password) to check they match.

Section Four — Selection

Section Five — Iteration

for Loops

> **Learning Objectives**
>
> Off we go again, it's time to learn another new thing. Iteration is all about repeating an action within code and we'll take a look at this before diving into for loops...
>
> - Understand the purpose of iteration in algorithms.
> - Learn how to represent iteration in a flowchart.
> - Understand the purpose of the for loop.
> - Learn how to use for in count programs and to print characters.
> - Learn how to use a nested for loop in a program.
> - Understand that loops can make programming more robust.

Iteration is a process of repeating instructions

1) As mentioned in Section Four, proper programs are made from combinations of three building blocks — sequence, selection and iteration.
2) In the book so far, you've seen sequencing and selection — now it's time to take a look at iteration.
3) Iteration means to loop or repeat an action within a program. You'll see the terms iteration and loop used interchangeably.

Iteration can be shown as a flowchart

A flowchart shows the flow of data through the algorithm.

EXAMPLE

The example below shows the line "Hip Hip Hooray!" being repeated three times.

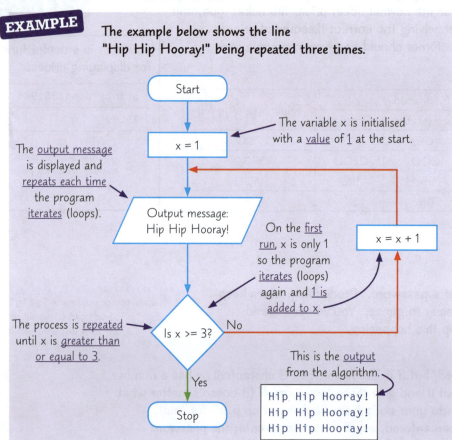

- The variable x is initialised with a value of 1 at the start.
- The output message is displayed and repeats each time the program iterates (loops).
- On the first run, x is only 1 so the program iterates (loops) again and 1 is added to x.
- The process is repeated until x is greater than or equal to 3.
- This is the output from the algorithm.

Q1 Draw your own flowchart, replacing the message in the example with a repeated song lyric of your choice.

Make sure to specify how many times it repeats (iterates).

REAL WORLD CODE

Devices like smart speakers, computer games and electronic toys can use iteration with snippets of recorded audio. Each word or phrase only needs to be recorded once, but can be repeated lots of times.

for Loops

A for loop repeats a certain number of times

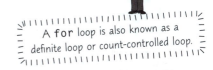

EXAMPLE Here's a simple for loop.

The variable i can be <u>anything</u>. You'll find i is often used as it's <u>short for index</u>.

The <u>indented line</u> after the colon is what is <u>repeated</u>.

```
for i in range(5):
    print(i)
0
1
2
3
4
```

The range function is used to <u>generate a sequence</u> of numbers, starting at <u>zero</u>.

The <u>colon</u> is essential as it will <u>indent</u> the next line. Without it a <u>syntax error</u> will occur.

This loop will iterate <u>five times</u> to create the output shown (0, 1, 2, 3, 4).

The upper limit of any range isn't included. For example, a range of 11 will finish at 10.

A for loop is also known as a definite loop or count-controlled loop.

A for loop can be used to <u>recreate</u> the example on the previous page.

The print statement indented <u>below</u> the for loop can display <u>any message</u>.

```
for i in range(3):
    print("Hip Hip Hooray!")
```

Hip Hip Hooray!
Hip Hip Hooray!
Hip Hip Hooray!

EXAMPLE A starting number can also be added to the range function.

```
for i in range(2,5):
    print(i)
2
3
4
```

A <u>starting number of 2</u> has been added followed by a comma. This means that the range will <u>start at 2</u> and then <u>stop</u> before reaching 5.

Q2 Edit the range function in the example program on the left to output the values 1-5.

for loops can be used in variety of ways

1) A <u>third value</u> can be added to the range function that defines the <u>step</u> of each iteration.

EXAMPLE Adding the value -1 will generate a decreasing sequence that i will iterate through.

```
for i in range(5,0,-1):
    print(i)
5
4
3
2
1
```

These numbers show this loop <u>starts</u> at 5, <u>stops</u> before reaching 0 and <u>decreases</u> by 1 after each iteration.

Q3 Complete the output for the iteration below.

```
for i in range(100,0,-25):
    print(i)
```

2) Iteration can also be used to loop through a string <u>one character</u> at <u>a time</u>.

```
word = "wheels"
for char in word:
    print(char)
w
h
e
e
l
s
```

This style of for loop is sometimes called a 'for-each' loop. You'll see these in Section Six.

Q4 Create a similar program but skip the 'e' characters.

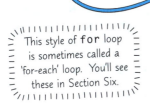
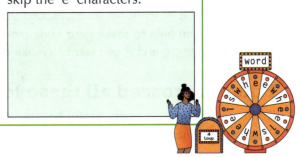

Section Five — Iteration

for Loops

A nested for loop places one loop inside another

1) In a nested for loop each iteration of the outer loop causes the inner loop to run until complete.
2) Imagine you have a for loop that iterates a set number of times. If the inner loop repeats m times and the outer loop repeats n times then, in total, the code in the inner loop will repeat m x n times.

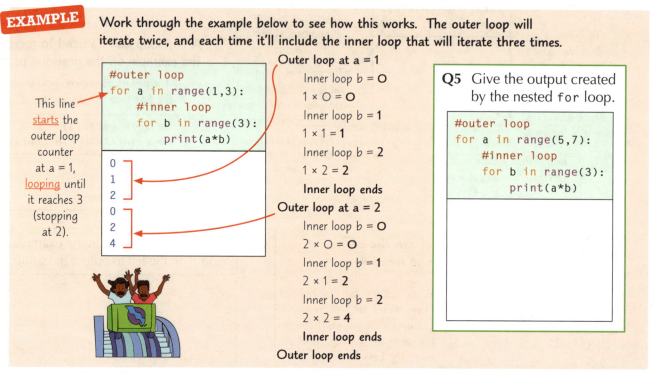

EXAMPLE Work through the example below to see how this works. The outer loop will iterate twice, and each time it'll include the inner loop that will iterate three times.

```
#outer loop
for a in range(1,3):
    #inner loop
    for b in range(3):
        print(a*b)
```

This line starts the outer loop counter at a = 1, looping until it reaches 3 (stopping at 2).

Output:
0
1
2
0
2
4

Outer loop at a = 1
Inner loop b = 0
1 × 0 = 0
Inner loop b = 1
1 × 1 = 1
Inner loop b = 2
1 × 2 = 2
Inner loop ends
Outer loop at a = 2
Inner loop b = 0
2 × 0 = 0
Inner loop b = 1
2 × 1 = 2
Inner loop b = 2
2 × 2 = 4
Inner loop ends
Outer loop ends

Q5 Give the output created by the nested for loop.

```
#outer loop
for a in range(5,7):
    #inner loop
    for b in range(3):
        print(a*b)
```

3) The number of times a for loop iterates can also change based on a variable elsewhere in the program.

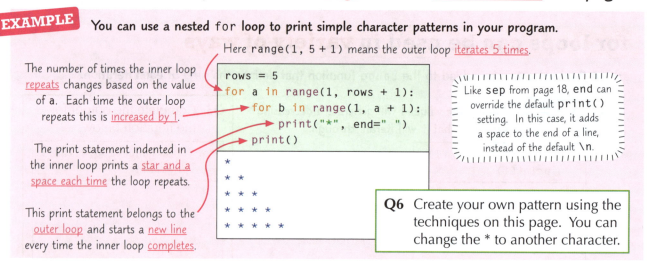

EXAMPLE You can use a nested for loop to print simple character patterns in your program.

Here range(1, 5 + 1) means the outer loop iterates 5 times.

```
rows = 5
for a in range(1, rows + 1):
    for b in range(1, a + 1):
        print("*", end=" ")
    print()
```

The number of times the inner loop repeats changes based on the value of a. Each time the outer loop repeats this is increased by 1.

The print statement indented in the inner loop prints a star and a space each time the loop repeats.

This print statement belongs to the outer loop and starts a new line every time the inner loop completes.

Output:
```
*
* *
* * *
* * * *
* * * * *
```

Like sep from page 18, end can override the default print() setting. In this case, it adds a space to the end of a line, instead of the default \n.

Q6 Create your own pattern using the techniques on this page. You can change the * to another character.

Loops can help make programs more robust

1) Loops can save you time when writing code because you're not having to write the same instructions over and over again.
2) Loops also help to make your code more robust. As there's less code, it reduces the likelihood of coding errors and if you want to make changes to the code you don't need to change it in multiple places.

Fingers crossed all these loops don't make you dizzy...

Remember, loops are really useful because they allow you to have code that repeats but is only present in the program once. This means it's quicker to write and you're less likely to introduce erors, oops, errors.

Section Five — Iteration

Practice Questions and Activities

Q1 Complete the flowchart on the right so it will create the output shown.

```
We love you Python, we do.
We love you Python, we do.
We love you Python, we do.
We love you Python, we do.
```

Q2 Give the output for each program.

a)
```
for x in range(6):
    print(x)
```

b)
```
for y in range(10,14):
    print(y)
```

Q3 Describe what adding a third value within the `range` function in a `for` loop will do.

....

....

Q4 Describe what a nested `for` loop is.

....

....

Q5 Complete the following questions about the example code given.

```
for s in range(1,4):
    for t in range(4):
        print(s*t)
```

a) State the line that starts the inner loop.

....

b) State the line that starts the outer loop.

....

c) How many times will the inner loop iterate in total?

....

d) List, in order, the outputs that would be generated by the code.

....

Q6 Describe two benefits of making a program more robust using a loop.

....

....

....

Section Five — Iteration

while Loops

> **Learning Objectives**
>
> With `while` loops you're saying to Python: "I need you to keep doing this important thing, but only while this other important thing is true".
> - Understand the purpose of condition-controlled loops.
> - Learn how to represent a while loop in a flowchart.
> - Understand the difference between the `while` and `for` loop.
> - Learn how to use a conditional `while` loop in a program.
> - Learn how to combine `while` and `else` in a program.

An indefinite loop depends on a condition

1) The `for` examples on p.43-44 iterated a specified number of times — this is called a definite loop.
2) An indefinite loop, or condition-controlled loop, continues until a specific condition is met or broken — this might involve looping twice, a million times or any other number of times.
3) In Python there's only one choice of indefinite loop — the `while` loop.

An indefinite loop can be shown as a flowchart

EXAMPLE

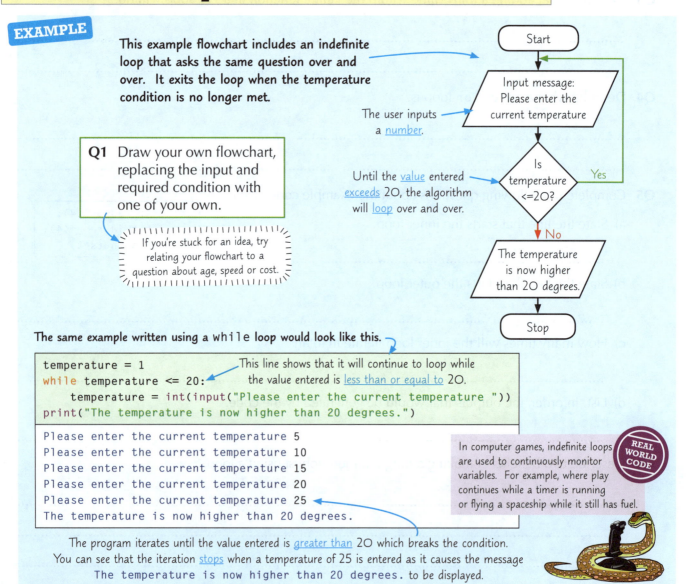

This example flowchart includes an indefinite loop that asks the same question over and over. It exits the loop when the temperature condition is no longer met.

The user inputs a number.

Until the value entered exceeds 20, the algorithm will loop over and over.

Q1 Draw your own flowchart, replacing the input and required condition with one of your own.

If you're stuck for an idea, try relating your flowchart to a question about age, speed or cost.

The same example written using a `while` loop would look like this.

```
temperature = 1
while temperature <= 20:
    temperature = int(input("Please enter the current temperature "))
print("The temperature is now higher than 20 degrees.")
```

This line shows that it will continue to loop while the value entered is less than or equal to 20.

```
Please enter the current temperature 5
Please enter the current temperature 10
Please enter the current temperature 15
Please enter the current temperature 20
Please enter the current temperature 25
The temperature is now higher than 20 degrees.
```

In computer games, indefinite loops are used to continuously monitor variables. For example, where play continues while a timer is running or flying a spaceship while it still has fuel.

REAL WORLD CODE

The program iterates until the value entered is greater than 20 which breaks the condition. You can see that the iteration stops when a temperature of 25 is entered as it causes the message `The temperature is now higher than 20 degrees.` to be displayed.

Section Five — Iteration

while Loops

You've seen a `while` loop in action already, but there are lots of other things they can be used for. Here are a couple of examples to get stuck into.

while loops can also be used for counting

1) Like `for` loops, `while` loops can be used to count up or down.
2) But you need to set the start point as a variable before the loop and use the end point in the condition. E.g. starting at 4 and ending at 0.
3) The example on the right uses -=. This is an assignment operator that subtracts the value on the right from the value of the variable and reassigns the result to the variable.
4) The assignment operator can also be written n = n - 1 as shown in the example below where n is the variable countdown.

```
n = 4
while n >= 0:
    print(n)
    n -= 1

4
3
2
1
0
```

`for` loops were used for counting on page 43.

EXAMPLE This example program is for a fairground ride countdown.

The starting value is initialised here.

The countdown continues while the value printed is greater than zero.

```
print("Get ready to ride")
countdown = 5
while countdown > 0:
    print(countdown)
    countdown = countdown - 1
print("Blast off!")
```

```
Get ready to ride
5
4
3
2
1
Blast off!
```

Q2 Adapt the fairground example to create the following output. Your program should contain a `while` loop.

```
Jump on three!
1
2
3
Jump!
```

while loops can keep going forever and ever and ever...

Take care to ensure that your `while` loop condition will eventually become `False` — if it doesn't then you could be stuck in an infinite loop.

CODE ERRORS A common mistake is not giving the user a chance to re-enter an input.

Here, the idea is to keep looping until the value of marks is within the valid range (0 to 100).

However, when a value outside of this range, e.g. 133, is entered the line "Mark is invalid." will be repeated continuously.

```
marks = int(input("Mark entry: "))

while not(0 <= marks <= 100):
    print("Mark is invalid.")
```

```
Mark entry: 133
Mark is invalid.
Mark is invalid.
Mark is invalid.
Mark is invalid.
Mark is invalid.
Mark is invalid.
Mark is invalid.
Mark is invalid.
Mark is invalid.
```

The logic error here is that the value of `marks` never changes — and so the loop condition will never change from `True` to `False`.

This loop is 'infinite' as it won't end until the user forces it to or it crashes.

Don't panic if you make a loop infinite by mistake — close the window or in IDLE, use the shortcut CTRL + C to terminate it.

Modifying the loop to give the user another go at changing `marks` fixes this.

```
marks = int(input("Mark entry: "))

while not(0 <= marks <= 100):
    print("Mark is invalid.")
    marks = int(input("Mark entry: "))
```

while Loops

You can end a loop early with break

1) break is a simple but powerful command which can be useful within loops — when it's executed, the loop that it's inside will immediately end.
2) You can use break in both for and while loops.
3) Below is an example that requires indefinite iteration.

EXAMPLE   This PIN checker keeps iterating until the PIN matches.

The actual PIN is set at the start.

This condition will never become False, but the loop is not infinite as break is used as an alternative way to end it.

```
pin = "1977"

while True:
    userPin = input("Enter your 4-digit PIN: ")

    if userPin == pin:
        print("PIN correct, you may proceed.")
        break
```

```
Enter your 4-digit PIN: 0000
Enter your 4-digit PIN: 1234
Enter your 4-digit PIN: 1977
PIN correct, you may proceed.
```

Using break at the end of while True means the loop body always runs at least once.

Remember == means 'exactly equal to'.

When 1977 is entered, the if condition is True and so break runs which ends the loop.

Q3 Adapt this example so that a message is shown to the user to tell them when they enter an incorrect PIN.

Q4 Modify your Q3 program so that break isn't needed.

else can be used with loops that break

1) With loops, else is used to contain code that will run only if the loop ends normally.
2) 'Normally' means that the loop ended because of the count or condition and not because of a break statement — break makes it abnormal.

EXAMPLE   This adapts the code above so that the user only has 3 attempts to get the PIN correct.

After each guess, 1 is added to the current value of attempt. When it reaches 3, the while condition is no longer true.

+= adds a value to an existing variable (here it's attempt) and assigns the resulting total value to the variable.

This else clause belongs to while not if. It will only run if the loop ends normally — in this case that's after 3 attempts.

```
pin = "1977"
attempt = 0

while attempt < 3:
    userPin = input("Enter your 4-digit PIN: ")
    attempt += 1

    if userPin == pin:
        print("PIN correct, you may proceed.")
        break

else:
    print("You are out of attempts.")
```

```
Enter your 4-digit PIN: 0000
Enter your 4-digit PIN: 1234
Enter your 4-digit PIN: 5555
You are out of attempts.
```

Q5 Rewrite the while loop in this example as a for loop.

If the entered value matches pin, the user is told the PIN is correct and the loop ends due to the break. The code in the else clause would not be run.

When the user has entered the incorrect PIN 3 times, the condition of the while loop becomes False. This stops the iteration and else runs instead.

Consider yourself lucky the jokes aren't looping indefinitely...

Make sure your while loop has a break or a condition that will turn False or it'll keep running forever. Remember, this is different to for loops which only iterate a definite number of times before they stop.

Practice Questions and Activities

Q1 a) What name is given to the Python loop that implements indefinite iteration?

....

b) Describe the difference between a definite and an indefinite loop.

....

....

Q2 Give the next message output to the user after each of these inputs into the program.

a) Input: 6

Output: ....

....

```
temp = 1
while temp >= 0:
    temp = int(input("Please enter the current water temperature "))
print("The water should now be frozen.")
```

b) Input: -4

Output: ....

Q3 Describe the purpose of adding an `else` clause to a simple `while` (or `for`) loop.

....

....

Q4 Write a counting program for each output below. Each program should contain a `while` loop.

a)

```
9
8
7
6
```

b)

```
10
11
12
13
```

Q5 Use a while loop to meet the following criteria.

- The user is asked to type in the value of π rounded to three decimal places.

- When the user gets it wrong, the question is asked again.

- This repeats until 3.142 (π to three decimal places) is entered and the message "Correct" is outputted.

> Remember to use the correct data type for decimal numbers. Take a look at Section Three for a reminder.

Coding Challenges for Section Five

Great work, you've made it to the end of another section. Now it's time to tackle some coding challenges. Once you've had a go visit the link on the contents page to download example programs for each challenge.

Challenge 1

As part of an online quiz game, you have been asked to write some code that displays a bonus points score.

Your program should:
- Have the score start at 1 000 000 and counts down in steps of 100 000, all the way to 0.
- Have a message saying "Bonus points lost" at the end of the countdown.

Challenge 2

As part of a film review website, you have been asked to program a small graphic that displays star ratings. The pattern required is shown below.

You have been advised to use a nested `for` loop for this, rather than a straight printed output as the pattern and number of stars may change in the future.

Challenge 3

A website describes the location of well-maintained mountain bike routes across the Peak District. To access the website, users must login with an email address and 8-character password.

You have been asked to write a small program that checks the email address and 8-character password match the ones that are stored in the program.

Your program should:
- Make use of the following sample account details.

  ```
  The email address: tariq@azmail.co.uk
  The password is: P_5*K1@8
  ```

- Only allow the customer to attempt their username and password four times, after that the login program will end.
- Only allow access to the website if both the email address and password are correct (i.e. they match the sample account details).

Hint: Think about what Boolean operator might be useful.

Challenge 4

You've been asked by a primary school teacher to write a program to help with learning times tables.

The teacher would like the program to work in the following way:
- The user is asked to type in which times table they want to start from (e.g. 7 will start at the 7 times table).
- Starting at 0 and continuing upwards, the user should be asked for the times table answer (e.g. 7 * 0 =).
- The current times table sequence ends when the user types "Done". Then the next times table up should begin (e.g. 8 * 0 =).
- When the user wants to end the program, they type "Finished" and then the number of questions they got right and wrong should be printed.

Section Six — Data Structures

Lists

> **Learning Objectives**
> Make sure you've got your head around Section Five before you start this one. There's loads of data coming your way and those loops will save you a bunch of time.
> - Understand what a data structure is.
> - Be able to create lists and use indices.
> - Be able to use some useful list methods.

Data structures are used to group multiple items

1) So far, variables have been used to store single data values.
2) For example, if I wanted to keep track of all my friends, I could assign each of their names to similarly named variables.
3) This isn't very efficient or readable — it'd be much better to group them together in a single variable. That's what a data structure is — an organised collection of items.
4) In Python, the built-in data structures are lists, tuples, sets and dictionaries.
5) Different data structures use different approaches to arrange the items. It's a bit like people having a variety of storage units at home — each one has a slightly different intended use and has its own pros and cons.

```
friend1 = "Alice"
friend2 = "Bob"
friend3 = "Chuma"
friend4 = "Delia"
friend5 = "Eve"
```

Lists can contain multiple items stored under one name

1) Lists are created using square brackets and have commas separating the different data values.
2) Lists are assigned to variables in the normal way — with a variable name and an equals sign.
3) On its own, the variable name will output all the list items at once, which doesn't look great and isn't that useful.

```
# Initialising a list with 5 items.
friends = ["Alice","Bob","Chuma","Delia","Eve"]

# Printing the contents of the list.
print("My pals are",friends)
```
```
My pals are ['Alice', 'Bob', 'Chuma', 'Delia', 'Eve']
```

The naming rules for variables (see p.14) apply here too.

Lists are indexed just like strings

1) To get an individual item held within a list, use the index number as you did for characters within strings (see p.29-30).
2) The first item has index zero and the indices count upwards from this.
3) You can use the index to change a particular item.
4) A list is like a box with individual compartments — each of which has an index number to label it.

```
# Continuation of the code from above.

print("My first friend was",friends[0] + "...")
friends[2] = "Aisha"
print("My best mates are",friends[4],"and",friends[2])
```
```
My first friend was Alice…
My best mates are Eve and Aisha
```

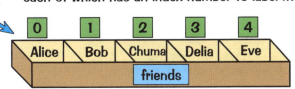

Someone not a friend anymore? Use `del friends[i]` to remove them, replacing i with the index of the friend you're removing.

Lists

Lists can contain items of multiple data types

1) In the `friends` list, all the items were strings, but a mix of data types can be used.
2) If you're studying GCSE Computer Science, there's a good chance you'll encounter a data structure called an 'array'. Python doesn't have built-in support for arrays so lists are often used instead.
3) The main difference between an array and a list is that arrays typically don't allow the items to be different data types — so lists in Python are a bit more flexible.

Q1 Give four basic data types in Python.

Indexing is only ever a digit away from disaster

Here are some examples of errors that can occur when indexing.

```
shopping = ["Apples",4,"Bananas",5,"Croissants",10]
print("I need to get",shopping[6],shopping[5])
IndexError: list index out of range
```

This error shows up when you're trying to index an item that doesn't exist. There's no index 6 — despite the length of the list being 6 items, always remember to start counting from 0.

This is a specific version of the same error — it happens when you try to assign an item to an index that doesn't exist. Line 4 is trying to add the next prime number to the list but unless there's an item there already, the program can't do it. For this you should use `.append()` instead — see below.

```
primes = [2,3,5,8]
primes[-1] = 7
print(primes)
primes[4] = 11
[2, 3, 5, 7]
IndexError: list assignment index out of range
```

Remember, an index of -1 refers to the last value.

List methods save you time

Data structures come with built-in methods that are designed to help programmers do common jobs. This table has some of the most useful list methods.

For now, think of methods as functions that apply directly to an object such as a list.

Method	Purpose	In Action	Explanation

`.append()`	To add a new item to the end of the list.	`primes = [2,3,5,7]`
		`print("Before: ",primes)`
		`primes.append(11)`
		`print("After: ",primes)`
		
		`Before: [2, 3, 5, 7]`
		`After: [2, 3, 5, 7, 11]`
			Here's `.append()` being used to get around the `IndexError` given with the `primes` example above. Since it's a method, it directly follows the `primes` name after a full stop and adds the item without needing an equals sign to assign it.

`.insert()`	To add a new item to a specified position in the list.	`buses = ["31","5","63","331"]`
		`buses.insert(2,"U9")`
		`buses.remove("31")`
		`print("Fleet:",len(buses),"buses")`
		`print("Latest:",buses[-1])`
		`print("All:",buses)`
		
		`Fleet: 4 buses`
		`Latest: 331`
		`All: ['5', 'U9', '63', '331']`
			`.insert()` is like a precise version of `.append()`, so you first need to give it the index of where you want the item to slot into. When it's first inserted, the U9 bus has index 2. However, by the time the final line is printed, it's slipped to index 1. That's because `.remove()` deleted bus 31, causing the other items to shuffle down by one position so that there are no gaps.

`.remove()`	To delete the item specified.		

`.index()`	To find the index of a specific item.	`chars = ["?","a","D","%","a"]`
		`print("Index of a:",chars.index("a"))`
		
		`Index of a: 1`
			`.index()` gives you the index of the first instance of the item that it can find. However, if the item isn't there, you'll get a `ValueError` so be cautious.

Section Six — Data Structures

Practice Questions and Activities

Q1 Give two reasons why data structures are useful.

1 ....

2 ....

Q2 Give the outputs of the lines 02, 05 and 09 for this code snippet.

```
01  colours = ["red", "blue"]
02  print(colours[1])
03
04  colours.append("purple")
05  print(colours)
06
07  del colours[0]
08  colours.insert(1,"green")
09  print(colours[2])
```

....

....

....

....

Q3 Each of these code snippets produces an error when they run. Explain why the error occurs.

a)
```
print(artists[1])
artists = ["Monet", 15, "Dali", "Kahlo"]
```

....

....

....

b)
```
actors = ["Olivier", "Hepburn", "Streep"]
print(actors.index(Freeman))
```

....

....

....

Q4 Write one line of code that will do the following to a list called `planets`.

a) Delete the planet that exists at index 3.

....

b) Remove `Pluto` from the list (it must've been put there by mistake...).

....

c) Insert `Proxima b` to the list directly after where the planet `Luyten b` already is.

....

Q5 Write a `for` loop that generates and adds the first 10 numbers of the 9 times table to a list. 90 should be the last item.

Iterating Through Lists

Learning Objectives

It's time to combine two of my favourite things — loops and data structures. They go together like butter and toast, sunshine and holidays, rain and Cumbria...

- To be able to iterate through a list.
- To compare the use of a 'for-each' loop and a for loop which uses range() to iterate through a list.

You can use a for loop to iterate through list items

1) A for loop lets you run through the items in a list and do something with them, e.g. outputting each item.
2) The great thing about Python's for loop is that you don't need to worry about how big the list will be when the program is running.

EXAMPLE

Ask a user to keep entering the names of their band members until they type in Stop. Keep hold of these names and then afterwards print out the names on one output line.

```
01  print("""Enter your band member's names.
02  When you're done, type \"Stop\".""")
03  band = []
04  userInput = input()
05
06  while userInput != "Stop":
07      band.append(userInput)
08      userInput = input()
09
10  print("The band is... ",end="")
11  for name in band:
12      print(name,end=", ")
```

This line initialises the band list to be empty. You can't append (line 7) to a list that doesn't exist — this line is needed even though it has no items.

Give the user another chance to give input within while — otherwise it becomes a dreaded infinite loop.

The name variable initially takes the value of the item at index 0. In each iteration, it takes the value of the next item in the list. Notice that you don't need to initialise the name variable before using it in the loop, since the for loop does that for you.

This string is over two lines — when this happens, you need triple quotes. You might remember using triple quotes for 'multi-line comments' (see page 12) but they're also just big strings.

Until the user types in Stop, their inputs will keep getting added to the band list.

This goes through each item one by one — so this style of loop is sometimes called a for-each loop.

```
Enter your band member's names.
When you're done, type "Stop".
Tariq
Dave
Lucy
George
Stop
The band is... Tariq, Dave, Lucy, George,
```

To get the band members on one line, the default end line character, \n, has been overridden (see p.44 for a reminder about end=", ").

Q1 Modify the code so that the user specifies how many members are in the band before the names are typed in.

Sometimes a for loop with range() is a better choice

A for-each loop is useful for quick and simple situations. However, a for loop that uses the range function (see p.43-44) is best for when you want to make use of the index numbers.

EXAMPLE

```
band = ["Tariq","Dave","Lucy","George"]

for i in range(len(band)):
    print(band[i]," (",i+1,"/",len(band),")",sep="",end=", ")
```
```
Tariq (1/4), Dave (2/4), Lucy (3/4), George (4/4),
```

i is used here as the index number. The length of the list (4) is used to iterate through index positions 0 to 3.

This print() line is using the variable i to index the list (band[i]) and also to output the position of the member in band (i+1).

Since for-each doesn't let you use the indices within the loop, you'd need to set up a counter yourself. That's why using this version of for is better when the index number is needed.

Q2 Change the range() so only Tariq and Lucy are printed.
Q3 Modify the code to leave out the final comma.

2D Lists

Learning Objectives
Bored of using only one index number? Well, you're in luck. It's time to double up and explore a whole new dimension.
- Understand what two-dimensional lists are and when they could be used.
- To be able to use nested for loops to iterate through a 2D list.

A 2D list is a list of lists

1) The lists used so far have all been one-dimensional (1D) — all the items in a 1D list are single data values.
2) Sometimes, these 1D lists are too simple for real-life situations. E.g. if a programmer wants to hold the forenames and surnames of classmates in a 1D list.

```
register = ["Ahmed","Kolia","Angela","Hamer","Katherine","Kat","Hill"]
```

3) It's not clear that Ahmed's surname is Kolia, for instance, or that Kat is Katharine's preferred forename. To get round this lack of clarity, separate lists could be initialised for each of them.

```
name1, name2, name3 = ["Ahmed","Kolia"],["Angela","Hamer"],["Katherine","Kat","Hill"]
print(name2)
```
```
['Angela', 'Hamer']
```

4) However, this replicates the problem identified at the start of this section of having lots of similar variable names. It's hard to keep track of the variables you've used and you can't iterate through every separate variable.
5) A solution is to bring in a list of lists — that's what a two-dimensional (2D) list is.

You need two indices to access data values in a 2D list

EXAMPLE Using a 2D list to hold the names of pupils in a class register.

```
register = [["Ahmed","Kolia"],["Angela","Hamer"],["Katherine","Kat","Hill"]]
# Indexing the first sublist
print("The first pupil:", register[0])

# Indexing the second item in the third sublist
print("The third pupil's forename:", register[2][1])
# Adding an item to the second sublist
register[1].insert(1,"Ann")
print("The updated second pupil:", register[1])

# Appending a new person to the register
register.append(["Tony","Anderson"])
print("The register now has", len(register), "pupils.")
```
```
The first pupil: ['Ahmed', 'Kolia']
The third pupil's forename: Kat
The updated second pupil: ['Angela', 'Ann', 'Hamer']
The register now has 4 pupils.
```

To access an entire sublist, use one index number only.

Each 'item' of the register list is another list containing its own items — those inner lists are called sublists.

To access an item in a sublist — use the first index to identify which sublist and the second index to identify which item in the sublist.

To maintain the structure of the 2D list, append whole lists only.

The benefit of using a 2D list is that it clearly separates the individuals. When they were all lumped together in a 1D list, there was no clear distinction between them.

1) 2D lists make code easier to read — it's more obvious in the code above that each sublist is for one person.
2) For this reason, 2D lists make it easier to program later on. For instance, if a person's full forename is always index 0 in the sublists, you can change i in register[i][0] to access each person's full forename. The lack of structure in the 1D list at the top of the page makes this job so much harder.

Section Six — Data Structures

2D Lists

2D lists are perfect for representing tables

A table of information can be represented in Python using a 2D list.
Formatting the initialisation more like a table helps to visualise the 2 'dimensions'.

Month	Average Temperature (°C)		
	Year 1	Year 2	Year 3
June	15.8	14.7	15.3
July	18.2	17.9	15.9
August	18.3	19.2	17.3

```
avgTemp = [[15.8, 14.7, 15.3],
           [18.2, 17.9, 15.9],
           [18.3, 19.2, 17.3]]
```

Q1 What is the index of the sublist representing August? ....

Q2 What code would index 15.9? ....

REAL WORLD CODE: avgTemp is a special kind of 2D list called a matrix. This is because each sublist is of the same size. Matrices are used a lot in data analysis and machine learning — sometimes they'll contain millions of items.

Nesting is needed to cover those double indices

One for loop was sufficient for accessing all items when only one index was needed.
However, to access all of the items in a 2D list you'll need to nest one for loop within another.

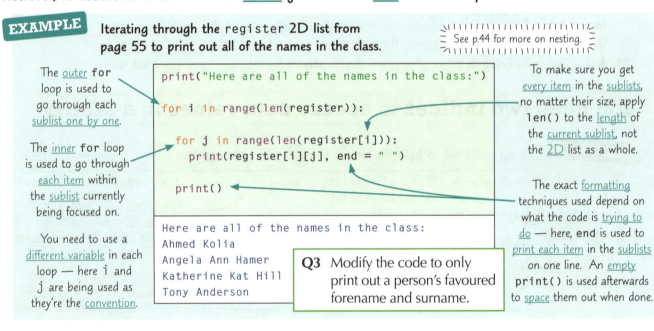

EXAMPLE Iterating through the register 2D list from page 55 to print out all of the names in the class.

See p.44 for more on nesting.

The outer for loop is used to go through each sublist one by one.

The inner for loop is used to go through each item within the sublist currently being focused on.

You need to use a different variable in each loop — here i and j are being used as they're the convention.

```
print("Here are all of the names in the class:")

for i in range(len(register)):

    for j in range(len(register[i])):
        print(register[i][j], end = " ")

    print()
```

```
Here are all of the names in the class:
Ahmed Kolia
Angela Ann Hamer
Katherine Kat Hill
Tony Anderson
```

To make sure you get every item in the sublists, no matter their size, apply len() to the length of the current sublist, not the 2D list as a whole.

The exact formatting techniques used depend on what the code is trying to do — here, end is used to print each item in the sublists on one line. An empty print() is used afterwards to space them out when done.

Q3 Modify the code to only print out a person's favoured forename and surname.

You can create multi-dimensional lists

1) It's possible to add more and more dimensions by creating more lists within lists.
2) There are more advanced situations when you might deal with data stretching across three dimensions, but these can often be held much more simply in a 2D list.

Adding additional dimensions is often unnecessary and can lead to your program becoming messy.

2D or not 2D — that is the question...

You might be feeling quite comfortable working in 1D, but don't limit yourself to it. Working in 2D fits more easily with many real life situations and is great when dealing with data that comes from a table.

Section Six — Data Structures

Practice Questions and Activities

Q1 How many times will line 5 in this code execute? Explain your answer.

```
01  pasta = ["Spaghetti","Penne",
02  "Tortelloni","Farfalle","Conchiglie"]
03  for shape in pasta:
04      if len(shape) > 6 or len(shape) < 9:
05          print(shape)
```

....

....

....

Q2 A 2D list is used to hold some events in British history. State the index (or indices) of the following items.

```
01  events = [["London is founded",50],
02             ["The Battle of Hastings occurs",1066],
03             ["Birth of Henry VIII",1491,"King for 36 years"],
04             ["Primary school is made compulsory in Scotland",1872],
05             ["London hosts the Olympics",1948,"Also hosted in 1908 and 2012"]]
```

a) `1066`

....

b) `["Primary school is made compulsory in Scotland, 1872"]`

....

c) `"Also hosted in 1908 and 2012"`

....

Q3 Explain why it's more appropriate to represent the list in Q2 as a 2D list rather than a 1D list.

....

....

....

Q4 The code on the right follows on from the `events` initialisation in Q2. It's used to output each event on one line.

```
06  for i in range(len(events)):
07      for j in range(len(events)):
08          print(events[i][j],end=". ")
09      print()
```

a) Explain why two `for` loops are needed to do this task, but Q1 only used one.

....

....

b) There's a bug in the code that causes a runtime error. What line is it on and how can it be fixed?

....

....

Q5 Give the effect of the following lines of code on this list.

`myList = [["a","b","c"],[1, 2, 3]]`

a) `myList.insert(1, ["A","B","C"])`

....

b) `del myList["0"]["2"]`

....

Section Six — Data Structures

Tuples

Learning Objectives

Lists will probably be the data structure you'll use the most in Python. However, it's really important to get to grips with tuples, sets and dictionaries too — they have their uses.

- To understand what a tuple is and how they are different from lists.
- Know what immutable means and why being this can be an advantage.

You'll encounter sets and dictionaries on the next couple of pages.

Think of tuples like lists that you want to keep fixed

1) The word 'tuple' comes from the suffix 'uple'. It appears in words like 'couple' and 'quadruple' which can be used to describe the size of tuples — e.g. a septuple would have seven items.

2) One difference between lists and tuples is that tuples use round brackets instead of square brackets.

```
# Initialising a list
myList = ["Ed",17,True,-12.5]

print(myList)
print("2nd item is",myList[1])
```
```
['Ed', 17, True, -12.5]
2nd item is 17
```

```
# Initialising a tuple
myTuple = ("Ed",17,True,-12.5)

print(myTuple)
print("2nd item is",myTuple[1])
```
```
('Ed', 17, True, -12.5)
2nd item is 17
```

The round brackets are just used for setting up the tuple.

Indexing works the exact same as with lists — including the use of square brackets and counting from 0.

3) A key difference between lists and tuples is that lists are mutable, whereas tuples are immutable.

4) An immutable data structure isn't changeable once set. So tuples can't be changed but lists can be.

CODE ERRORS — Trying to change a tuple doesn't work, although you can overwrite them.

```
myTuple = ("Ed",17,True,-12.5)
myTuple[0] = "Harry"
```
```
TypeError: 'tuple' object does not support item assignment
```

You can't add or change items.

```
myTuple = ("Ed",17,True,-12.5)
myTuple = ("Harry",17,True,-12.5)
print(myTuple)
```
```
('Harry', 17, True, -12.5)
```

But you can reassign a whole new tuple to the same variable name.

There are two methods that get used on tuples

Because tuples are immutable, it means that .append(), .insert(), .remove() and most of the other methods used on lists aren't needed. This leaves tuples with two built-in methods — .index() and .count().

```
europe = ("Hej","Hallo","Bonjour","Hallo","Hola","Salve","Hallo")
print("The Spanish \"Hello\" is at position", europe.index("Hola"))
print("\"Hallo\" is used by", europe.count("Hallo"), "European languages")
```
```
The Spanish "Hello" is at position 4
"Hallo" is used by 3 European languages
```

You've seen .index() before, but .count() returns the number of items in the tuple (or list) that match the value supplied.

Tuples being immutable can be useful

1) As they're immutable, once a tuple is initialised individual items can't be mistakenly changed later on.
2) For programs written by a single person, changes like this might not be a problem — but if you're dealing with code written by many people, there's a larger risk of side effects which could damage your code.
3) These side effects occur when some code unintentionally changes some values held in another part of the program — using tuples reduces the risk of this happening.

Possible side effects of using tuples: headaches, mutations...

You might've come across 'constants' when studying Computer Science. Constants exist in other languages but not Python. Tuples are arguably the closest thing, but constants can't usually be overwritten.

Sets

Learning Objectives

Under the bonnet, all of the data structures covered in this section use lots of maths and sets are the most mathsy of the bunch. Time to revisit some KS3 Maths...

- Understand what sets are and how they can be used.
- To be able to perform union, intersection, difference and symmetric difference.

Sets are chaotic compared to lists and tuples

1) A set is a data structure where the items are held with no clear order.
2) This means that sets, unlike lists and tuples, can't be indexed as the items appear to be arranged in an indecipherable order.
3) You can initialise sets with curly brackets and use methods to add or remove items.

```
mySet = {"a","b","c","d"}
print(mySet)
```
```
{'d', 'b', 'c', 'a'}
```
Notice how the items in the output appear in a different sequence to the initialisation.

```
mySet.add("e")
mySet.update({"f","g"})
mySet.remove("a")
print(mySet)
```
```
{'g', 'd', 'f', 'c', 'e', 'b'}
```

If you try the examples below, the order you see may well be different.

.add() adds one item only.

.update() can be used to add multiple items at once — these can be in set, list, tuple or dictionary form.

4) Another key difference between sets and the other data structures in Python is that the items in sets are unique — an item can't appear more than once in a set.
5) This uniqueness can be useful if you want to remove duplicates from lists or tuples.

```
prizeDraw = ["Jimmy","Jack","Jess","Jimmy","Jimmy","Jimmy"]
prizeDraw = set(prizeDraw)
prizeDraw = list(prizeDraw)
print("Pick a name from",prizeDraw)
```
```
Pick a name from ['Jimmy', 'Jack', 'Jess']
```
To remove repeated items from a list you can convert to a set and back again.

set() and list(), like tuple() and dict(), are used to convert between data structures — this is similar to the way int() and str() are used (see Section Three).

Set operations help you spot similarities and differences

Each of the following operations have their own methods and symbol operator (a symbol that represents the operation). For the following examples, assume x = {1, 2, 3, 4} and y = {3, 4, 5, 6}.

Operation	Purpose	In Action	Venn Diagram
Union (|)	To give all the items of both sets.	`print("All items:", x | y)` # Or: `print(x.union(y))` All items: {1, 2, 3, 4, 5, 6}	x{1,2,3,4} ∪ y{3,4,5,6}
Intersection (&)	To give only the items which appear in both sets.	`print("Matching items:", x & y)` # Or `print(x.intersection(y))` Matching items: {3, 4}	x ∩ y = {3,4}
Difference (-)	To give the items in one set but not in the other.	`print("In x but not in y:", x - y)` # Switching x and y does the converse In x but not in y: {1, 2}	x - y = {1,2}
Symmetric Difference (^)	To give all items except those that are in both.	`print("Items not in both:", x ^ y)` Items not in both: {1, 2, 5, 6}	{1,2,5,6}

Section Six — Data Structures

Dictionaries

> **Learning Objectives**
>
> One final data structure to cover and it's a real doozy (noun — Informal, North American — Something outstanding). I bet you're pretty excited to start so I'll let you get on...
> - To be able to initialise a dictionary with keys and values.
> - To be able to iterate through both the keys and values of a dictionary.

Dictionaries store data using key-value pairs

1) Dictionaries, like lists, can change items, add/remove items and make multi-dimensional data structures.
2) The main difference is that values in a dictionary are referenced using a key rather than an index. The keys can be any immutable data type such as a string, integer or even a tuple. The values can be anything.
3) A dictionary can be created with one item — it uses curly brackets and a colon between the key and the value. Additional items would be another key-value pair separated by a comma (see below).

```
example = {"key": "value"}
```
an item

EXAMPLE Using a dictionary to hold different acronyms and look-up some GCSE terms.

The jargon dictionary is initialised — the four comma-separated items could be put on one line, but separating them makes it more readable

```
jargon = {"IMAP": "Internet Message Access Protocol",
          "GUI": "Graphical User Interface",
          "TCP": "Transport Control Protocol",
          "RAM": "Random Access Memory"}

print("GUI stands for", jargon["GUI"])
```

Using the GUI key to lookup the associated value.

Dictionaries are mutable — so you can change values.

```
jargon["TCP"] = "Transmission Control Protocol"
print("TCP *actually* stands for", jargon["TCP"])
```

To add a new item, assign the value with a new key. There's no need for methods like .append() or .insert().

```
jargon["IDE"] = "Integrated Development Environment"
print("IDE has been added?", "IDE" in jargon)
```

The in keyword is great for checking if an item is in a data structure (either True or False). Here, it confirms that IDE has been added as a key.

```
GUI stands for Graphical User Interface
TCP *actually* stands for Transmission Control Protocol
IDE has been added? True
```

CODE ERRORS You've got to be careful with what you do with your keys.

A KeyError occurs when you try to get the value of a key that doesn't exist.

```
# Trying to index GUI
print(jargon["gui"])
```
```
KeyError: 'gui'
```

If you're not sure if a key exists use .get(). Worse case, it'll return None instead of ending your program.

```
print(jargon.get("gui"))
print(jargon.get("GUI"))
```
```
None
Graphical User Interface
```

You can loop through dictionaries using for loops

1) To get just the values from a dictionary, use .values(). For just the keys, use .keys().
2) You can also use the .items() method if you want to use both the key and the values.

```
for key in jargon.keys():
    print(key)
```
```
IMAP
GUI
TCP
RAM
IDE
```

```
for value in jargon.values():
    print(value)
```
```
Internet Message Access Protocol
Graphical User Interface
Transmission Control Protocol
```

```
for key, value in jargon.items():
    print(key, value)
```
```
IMAP Internet Message Access Protocol
GUI Graphical User Interface
TCP Transmission Control Protocol
```

They aren't shown here, but all five dictionary definitions would also be output for these examples.

Section Six — Data Structures

Practice Questions and Activities

Q1 What does it mean for a data structure to be immutable?

....

Q2 Draw lines to match up the name of each data structure to the properties it has. Some of the properties are shared by more than one.

Lists		Has built-in methods
		Immutable
Tuples		Uses curly brackets to initialise
		Items have no defined order
Sets		Indices can be custom
Dictionaries		Items must be unique

Q3 A supermarket runs a lunchtime meal deal. All drinks and snacks are included in the offer, but only the basic mains are. If a premium main is selected you'll need to pay full price. Sets are used to help work out the discounts.

```
basicMains = {"Sandwich","Pasta"}
premiumMains = {"Sushi","Caesar Salad","Pizza"}
drinks = {"Cola","Smoothie","Water"}
snacks = {"Granola","Chocolate","Crisps"}
```

   a) Write the result from `basicMains | premiumMains`.

   ....

   b) Write the result from `drinks & {"Iced Coffee","Water","Energy drinks","Smoothie"}`.

   ....

   c) A customer's shopping basket is held in a set called `selection`. Write an expression which uses set operations to select items in the basket that are eligible for the deal.

   ....

Q4 A network engineer uses a dictionary to map some domain names to their associated countries.

```
tld = {".uk": "United Kingdom",
       ".al": "Albania",
       ".co": "Colombia",
       ".pt": "Portugal",
       ".ml": "Mali"}
```

   a) Explain why a dictionary is a good choice for this situation.

   ....

   ....

   ....

   b) Give the items returned from `tld.keys()`.

   ....

   c) State the difference between doing `tld[".cn"]` and `tld.get(".cn")`.

   ....

   ....

Section Six — Data Structures

Coding Challenges for Section Six

It's challenge time again. These will give you a chance to test the knowledge you've gained from this section. Don't forget to visit the link on the contents page to download those handy Python programs.

Challenge 1

A new restaurant is launching with the tantalising menu shown on the right.

Arrange the relevant information from the menu into a data structure before showing this to the user as a presentable output.

Then give the user a couple of options:
- allow them to filter the menu to show only the vegetarian (V) options.
- allow them to filter the menu based on a price cut-off point they specify, i.e. to only show options below a certain price.

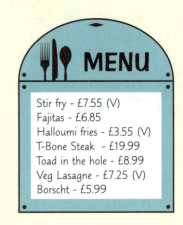

MENU

Stir fry - £7.55 (V)
Fajitas - £6.85
Halloumi fries - £3.55 (V)
T-Bone Steak - £19.99
Toad in the hole - £8.99
Veg Lasagne - £7.25 (V)
Borscht - £5.99

Challenge 2

A mathematician wants to study relationships between different numerical sequences. For reasons known only to her, the mathematician specifically wants to focus on odd numbers, multiples of 13, multiples of 16, and perfect numbers, but only those between 0 and 10 000.

For each of these sequences, generate the numbers that fall between 0 and 10 000. At this point, don't show these numbers to the user (the mathematician).

Once the numbers have been generated, show the mathematician the following:
- All of the perfect numbers generated in this range
- Ten examples of multiples of 13 that are also odd
- How many multiples of 13 there are that are not odd
- The numbers that are perfect and also multiples of 16

A number is 'perfect' if all of its factors (not including the number itself) add up to the number. E.g. 6 is a perfect number as its factors are 1, 2, and 3, and they add up to 6.

Challenge 3

A village cricket club has given up on asking volunteers to score their matches by hand. Instead, they want a program that will tally up the scores automatically.

> Skip this box if you don't need (or want) to know about cricket scoring. In cricket, a single over consists of 6 balls which are bowled at a batter. If the batter doesn't get a run when a ball is bowled, they score zero for that ball. The maximum number of runs they can get per ball is 6. An innings is how many overs one team is batting for. The team's final score is how many runs were scored in that innings.

The program should do the following:
- For each ball in an over, ask the user for how many runs were scored.
- If the user types in an invalid score, ask them for it repeatedly until the number of runs is in the correct range.
- After the over is finished, print out the runs scored across the over. For example:

  `Over 3: 0, 1, 4, 6, 4, 2`

- End the innings when 5 overs have been played.
- After the innings is finished, print out the team's final score. This should also contain a breakdown of each over's individual runs. For example:

  ```
  The final score was 76 runs.
  
  Over 1: 1, 0, 4, 6, 1, 2
  Over 2: 3, 1, 0, 0, 0, 0
  Over 3: 0, 1, 4, 6, 4, 2
  ...
  ```

The '...' is used to show that there'd be more results output which we haven't shown here.

Section Seven — Subroutines

Subroutines

Learning Objectives

In Python, subroutines can be described as functions, methods and procedures. This might not mean much now, but all will become clear over the next few pages...

- Understand what a subroutine is.
- Understand the purpose of subroutines.
- Understand how subroutines can be represented in a flowchart.

A subroutine is like a mini program

1) A subroutine is a named block of self-contained code which performs a specific task.
2) Self-contained means that a subroutine can run on its own — it shouldn't need to rely on code outside of it. As they're independent blocks of code, subroutines can be easily moved and reused in different programs.

Subroutines can also be called 'subprograms' or 'routines'.

Subroutines allow code to be efficiently repeated

1) When writing longer programs certain blocks of code may need to be used more than once.
2) This might be a currency converter, string conversion, displaying a main menu or printing a numerical sequence on screen.
3) Rather than repeating the same block of code over and over, it can be defined once as a subroutine and then called whenever you need it.
4) Python has many built-in subroutines — see the next page for a list of some of the built-in subroutines you've already used in this book.
5) It's also possible to create user-defined subroutines — these are covered on p.67-68.

Calling a subroutine is when you run its code.

Subroutines can be represented in flowcharts

Look at the algorithm below. The flowchart on the left asks the user their name and stores it as a variable. This flowchart represents a subroutine, which is then called in the flowchart on the right.

EXAMPLE Here's an example of how flowcharts can be used to show subroutines being called within another algorithm.

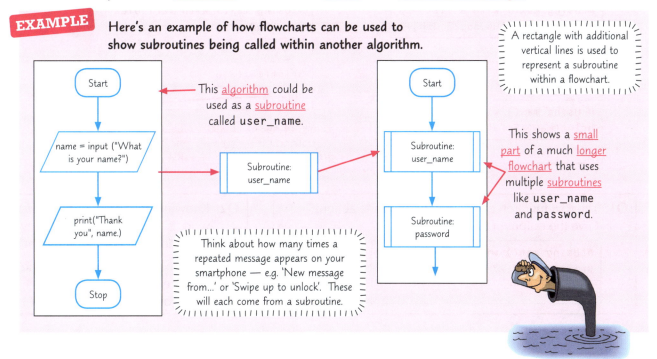

A rectangle with additional vertical lines is used to represent a subroutine within a flowchart.

This algorithm could be used as a subroutine called user_name.

This shows a small part of a much longer flowchart that uses multiple subroutines like user_name and password.

Think about how many times a repeated message appears on your smartphone — e.g. 'New message from...' or 'Swipe up to unlock'. These will each come from a subroutine.

Built-in Subroutines

Learning Objectives

Right from the start you've used subroutines — like using `print()` to output Hello World. Below are a few ready-made subroutines to recap before you start to make your own.

- Understand what built-in subroutines are and why they exist.
- Understand the difference between functions and methods.
- Revisit some of the important functions and methods already covered in this book.
- Understand the difference between a function and a procedure.

Built-in subroutines are ready to use

1) Python has two types of subroutines — functions and methods (see p.65). Here's a list of some of the functions that you've seen so far.
   - `print()` — used to display a message on screen.
   - `input()` — used to receive the user's response to a prompt.
   - `float()` — used to cast to a positive or negative number with a fractional part.
   - `str()` — used to cast any data to a string.
   - `len()` — used to check the length of something, e.g. the number of characters in a string.

2) The functions above are built-in — this means that the developers of Python have already written the code to do those tasks. You can run their code whenever you want by calling them.

3) When you call a function, Python executes the subroutine code that is held in one of the source files on your computer.

4) Built-in subroutines are a great way of saving time when programming as they're ready to use without you needing to do any coding.

REAL WORLD CODE — Python is open source, so the code for these built-in functions is published online. Not all of them are written in Python though — the language 'C' is often used because its code runs faster.

The max function returns the largest value in a sequence

EXAMPLE Two built-in functions are called in all of these examples — `print()` and `max()`.

```
# Using max() with a list
print(max([5,100,55,23,300]))
300
```

`print()` and `max()` are being called here.

```
# Using max() with a dictionary
print(max({5:"a",10:"b",3:"c"}))
10
```

```
# Using max() with variables
a = 5000
b = 500
c = 50
print(max(a,b,c))
5000
```

When `max()` finishes executing, the calling statement is replaced with the biggest value. `print()` is needed to display that result to the user.

Q1 The min function carries out the opposite action. Give the output of this code.

```
# Using min() with sets
print(min({2,-7,5}^{-7,2,3,14}))
```

See p.59 for more on ^.

Q2 Knowing how `max()` and `min()` work is useful, especially if they don't quite do the job for a particular task.

Write a program for each of the above examples that does the same job but doesn't use `max()`.

Built-in Subroutines

Methods work directly on objects

1) Methods are the second type of subroutine in Python. Examples of built-in methods you've used include:
   - `.append()` — used to add an item to the end of a list.
   - `.upper()` — used to convert all characters in a string to uppercase.
   - `.get()` — used to find the value from a dictionary when you provide its key.

   A visible difference between a function and a method is that there's a full stop before a method name.

2) Methods are designed to only work with something specific — this comes before the full stop and is called an object. For example, the get method would be called on a dictionary object named myDictionary with the line `myDictionary.get("My Key")`.

3) Most things are an object in Python — including variables, lists, sets, integers, Boolean values and almost everything else you've used so far. If something has its own methods, it's an object.

4) Functions like `print()` and `len()` work with a few different objects, whereas methods are pretty specific to the object they're designed to work with — for example, `.append()` only works with lists.

There's a built-in method and function to sort lists

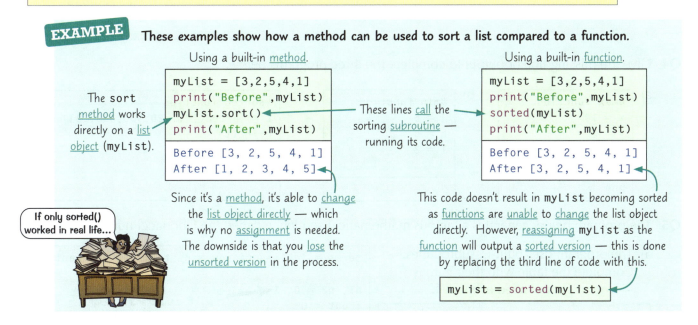

EXAMPLE These examples show how a method can be used to sort a list compared to a function.

Using a built-in method.

The sort method works directly on a list object (myList).

```
myList = [3,2,5,4,1]
print("Before",myList)
myList.sort()
print("After",myList)

Before [3, 2, 5, 4, 1]
After [1, 2, 3, 4, 5]
```

These lines call the sorting subroutine — running its code.

Since it's a method, it's able to change the list object directly — which is why no assignment is needed. The downside is that you lose the unsorted version in the process.

If only sorted() worked in real life...

Using a built-in function.

```
myList = [3,2,5,4,1]
print("Before",myList)
sorted(myList)
print("After",myList)

Before [3, 2, 5, 4, 1]
After [3, 2, 5, 4, 1]
```

This code doesn't result in myList becoming sorted as functions are unable to change the list object directly. However, reassigning myList as the function will output a sorted version — this is done by replacing the third line of code with this.

```
myList = sorted(myList)
```

Functions which don't return can be called procedures

1) In the example above, `sorted()` returned a sorted list (as you'd see after it's assigned) when it finished executing — that means it produced something we can use.

2) Not all functions do this. For example, `print()` doesn't return a value, it just displays a message.

```
valueReturned = print("This is a procedure.")
print(valueReturned)

This is a procedure.
None
```

3) If you try and use a `print()` call in an assignment, like the example above did with `sorted()`, you'll find that None is left there — which shows that nothing was returned.

4) Functions that don't return a value to the main program, like `print()` can be called procedures.

"Functions all live in a yellow sub-routine..."

Wow, that was intense. There have been plenty of important terms flying around on these pages. The important thing to remember is there are two key types of subroutines in Python — functions and methods.

Section Seven — Subroutines

Practice Questions and Activities

Q1 State two reasons for using a subroutine in a program.

1 ....

2 ....

Q2 Give two examples of built-in functions and methods.
Use examples that you've not encountered in this section so far.

a) Function 1 ....

Function 2 ....

b) Method 1 ....

Method 2 ....

Q3 Describe two differences between functions and methods.

1 ....

2 ....

Q4 Give the missing line or output to complete the three programs below.

a)
```
#max function
x = 10
y = 200
z = 50

200
```

b)
```
#min function
j = 5
k = 6
l = 3

3
```

c)
```
#sorted function
t = sorted([7,1,20,980,325,13])
print(t)


```

Q5 The program below generates a famous mathematical sequence called the Fibonacci numbers.

a) The program uses built-in subroutines. Complete the table with their names — you might not need every cell.

Function	Procedure	Method

The operator += is used to add a value to an existing variable and assign the resulting total value to the variable.

```
terms = int(input("How many terms do you want? "))

n1, n2 = 0, 1
count = 0
fibonacci = []
```
This is shorthand to assign multiple variables on one line

```
while count < terms:
    fibonacci.append(str(n1))
    nth = n1 + n2
    n1 = n2
    n2 = nth
    count += 1

print(", ".join(fibonacci))
```
See page 86 for more on .join().

```
How many terms do you want? 5
0, 1, 1, 2, 3
```

b) Explain what the code inside the while loop does.

....

....

....

....

User-defined Functions

Learning Objectives

The built-in functions won't always be able to meet the requirements of a programmer. This means that programmers sometimes need to create their own functions.

- Understand the need for user-defined functions.
- Learn how to use user-defined functions.

User-defined functions can be called upon when needed

1) More complex programs are easier to read and maintain if they are structured using functions you've defined yourself. A user-defined function is a function that doesn't already exist in Python but is written by you instead.

2) Functions are usually defined at the start of your program so that you can call them throughout. The definition should be out-of-line — this means it's not where you actually need to use the code.

EXAMPLE Defining and then calling a user-defined function named time_converter for converting a number of days to hours and minutes.

This is the function definition. The body of the function (lines 2-4) must be indented.

These lines are outside the definition — this part is the main program.

```
def time_converter():
    hours = days * 24
    minutes = hours * 60
    print("This is",hours,"hours or",minutes,"minutes")
days = int(input("Enter the number of days: "))
time_converter()
days = int(input("Enter the number of days again: "))
time_converter()
```

```
Enter the number of days: 10
This is 240 hours or 14400 minutes
Enter the number of days again: 12
This is 288 hours or 17280 minutes
```

You must have brackets after the name, even if they're empty. You also need a colon.

The time_converter function is called by writing its name and the brackets. When this happens, the program executes the code in the function definition, before going back to the calling line when done.

Some of the examples on this page and page 68 use global variables (see p.70-71) when it's best practice to use parameters and return values instead.

Functions can be named in the same way as variables, although to make them easier to spot we're going to switch to snake_case (see p.14).

3) The example above calls the function twice. If it wasn't defined, you'd need to copy and paste in the code twice, which is inefficient and repeating blocks of code over and over can lead to mistakes.

4) If you find a bug in the function code, you only need to fix the bug once in the function definition and it'll update the whole program.

CODE ERRORS There are a few things that can go wrong with function definitions.

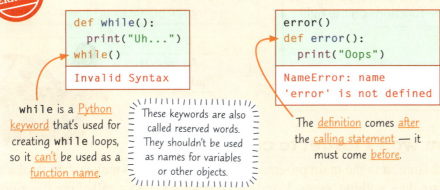

```
def while():
    print("Uh...")
while()
```
Invalid Syntax

while is a Python keyword that's used for creating while loops, so it can't be used as a function name.

These keywords are also called reserved words. They shouldn't be used as names for variables or other objects.

```
error()
def error():
    print("Oops")
```
NameError: name 'error' is not defined

The definition comes after the calling statement — it must come before.

```
def bungle():
    print("Oh dear :( ")
    bungle()
```

Nothing happens here as the calling statement is inside the definition (as it's still indented). Make sure you call in the main program or it won't actually run.

Section Seven — Subroutines

User-defined Functions

Functions are best defined for tasks that will be used a lot

EXAMPLE This program to generate an employee's ID code makes use of a user-defined function.

The variable surname is converted to uppercase and only the first four letters are used.

The identity code is shown when the function id_code is called and line 4 executes.

```
def id_code():
    upperSurname = surname.upper()
    ID = upperSurname[0:4] + yearOfBirth
    print(ID)

surname = input("Input surname: ")
yearOfBirth = input("Enter year of birth: ")
id_code()
```

```
Input surname: Anderson
Enter year of birth: 1999
ANDE1999
```

REAL WORLD CODE There are plenty of people that are now over 100 years old. In the past, many systems would only ask for the last two digits of the year of birth, but this can cause potential errors — e.g. 1922 and 2022. Always work with full years in four digits.

Q1 Give two reasons why defining a function for generating ID codes, as done in the example above, would be worth doing in a company with a large number of employees.

 CODE ERRORS An example of a common logic error is forgetting the brackets when trying to call a function.

```
# Alternative main program for example above
surname = input("Input surname: ")
yearOfBirth = input("Enter year of birth: ")
id_code
```

```
Input surname: Anderson
Enter year of birth: 1999
```

The function never runs because id_code is just the function's name. It isn't properly called until brackets are added, i.e. id_code().

To try and fix the error of the code not doing anything, a programmer might put it in a print() instead:

```
print(id_code)
```

```
<function id_code at 0x00000227F619FDC0>
```

This weird looking output is because Python is printing what the function is (to it) rather than running its code. The long hexadecimal number at the end of the output is usually the address of where the computer is holding it in memory.

A program can contain any number of subroutines

1) Larger programs may contain many subroutines.
2) Often these functions will be reused in multiple similar programs too.
3) These three functions could each be used within a larger program.

```
def chorus():
    print("ee-aye, ee-aye, oh!")
```

```
def farm():
    print("And on that farm he had a dog")
```

```
def intro():
    print("Old MacDonald had a farm")
```

Q2 Write the output from the following program assuming it uses the three functions on the right.

```
intro()
chorus()
farm()
chorus()
```

Ah, about that function...

Promise me that you won't forget to call...

Forgetting to call the function definition in the main program is an easy mistake to make when you're new to programming. If your program does nothing, go back and check whether you've called the function.

Section Seven — Subroutines

Practice Questions and Activities

Q1 Where are functions usually defined within a program? Explain why they are defined there.

....

....

Q2 Why isn't it possible to use the names `print` or `if` for user-defined functions?

....

....

Q3 Identify the two errors in the code on the right that are preventing it from doing what it's supposed to.

....

....

....

....

```
def main_menu():
    print("1. Start program.")
    print("2. Help guide.")
    print("3. Quit.")
main_menu
```

Q4 The three snippets of code below produce errors when they run. Rewrite each code snippet so that no error is produced when run.

a)
```
goldilocks()

def goldilocks():
    porridge = "hot"
    print(porridge)
```
`NameError: name 'goldilocks' is not defined`

b)
```
def get_postCode()
    postCode = input("Enter postcode")
    print(postCode)

get_postCode()
```
`Invalid syntax`

c)
```
def twelve():
for i in range(1,11):
   print(12*i)

twelve()
```
`Syntax Error: expected an indented block`

Q5 Describe the flow of execution in the code snippet below.

```
01  print("-"*20)
02
03  def welcome():
04      name = input("Hi! You are...")
05      print("Welcome",name)
06
07  welcome()
08  print("Let's begin.")
```

....

....

....

....

....

....

`*` can also be used to repeat strings — as seen on line 01 in the code above.

Section Seven — Subroutines

Global and Local Variables

Learning Objectives

Next up it's time to delve into the world of local variables, global variables and scope. Learning about scope is important as you start using more and more user-defined functions.

- Understand what scope is and the difference between a global and a local variable.
- Learn about how Python handles global and local variables and examples of bad practice.
- Understand the concept of a constant in programming.

Scope determines what your program can access

1) When you name an object in Python (like a variable, function or data structure) it's given a scope.
2) There are two main scopes used in Python: global and local scope.
3) Objects are only visible (and usable) to the parts of the program they are in the same scope with.
4) The rules and examples below deal with the scope of variables, but these rules apply to other objects too.
5) Here are some rules that determine whether a variable has global or local scope.

- If a variable is assigned inside a function definition, its scope is local to that function. → This means it can only be accessed by that function.
- If a variable is assigned outside all definitions (i.e. in the main program), its scope is global. → This means it can be accessed by the whole program.

EXAMPLE In this program the variable `test` has been assigned twice — once locally and once globally.

```
def function1():
    print("Print #2:",test)
def function2():
    test = 220
    print("Print #3:",test)

# Main program
test = 25
print("Print #1:",test)
function1()
function2()
print("Print #4:",test)
```

```
Print #1: 25
Print #2: 25
Print #3: 220
Print #4: 25
```

The prints have been labelled #1 to #4 to show the order they have been executed in.

This `test` is a global variable, as it's assigned outside of any function definition. The first `print()` line outputs 25, as you'd expect.

`function1` uses the global variable `test`, so 25 is printed when the function is called. As it's global, the function can access and use its value.

This `test` is a local variable as it's assigned inside a function. Local variables only exist while the function is executing, so this `test` doesn't exist when `function2` ends.

`function2` prints out the local variable `test`, which has the value 220. The global variable `test` still exists during this, but local variables always take priority. This means Python won't use the global variable if there's a local one with the same name.

The final `print()` line in the main program uses the global variable `test` because the value 220 only exists during `function2`'s execution.

CODE ERRORS Working with global and local variables can be confusing — here are some errors you might see.

This `test` is local to function and doesn't exist outside of the function. This is why trying to access it in the main program doesn't work.

```
def function():
    test = 955
function()
print(test)
```

```
NameError: name 'test'
is not defined
```

```
def function():
    print(test)
    test = 955
test = 92
function()
```

Even though there's a global `test`, because there's a local `test` assigned in the function, Python assumes you're trying to use the local one. As it hasn't got a value yet, it leads to an error.

```
UnboundLocalError: local variable 'test'
referenced before assignment
```

Section Seven — Subroutines

Global and Local Variables

Declare as global to change global variables in a function

1) As `function1` on the previous page shows, you can <u>access</u> global variables from <u>inside a function</u>.
2) But as `function2` shows, you can't <u>modify</u> global variables from <u>within a function</u>. If you try to, you'll either get an <u>error</u> or create a <u>local variable</u> instead.
3) To <u>stop</u> Python creating a <u>local variable</u>, you could use the `global` keyword <u>within the defined function</u> to <u>declare</u> the variable as <u>global</u>.

Declarations tell the program properties of objects (like their size or data type) before they're used. In Python, this is only needed for scope.

EXAMPLE Here's an example of how you can declare `test` as global.

You need to <u>declare</u> on a <u>separate line</u> before you assign it. Use the <u>global keyword</u> followed by the variable name.

<u>Calling</u> the function causes the <u>program flow</u> to jump up to Line 2, before <u>returning</u> back after Line 3 is <u>finished</u>.

```
01  def function():
02      global test
03      test = 220
04
05  test = 25
06  print("Print #1:",test)
07  function()
08  print("Print #2:",test)

Print #1: 25
Print #2: 220
```

This `test` is now referring to the same `test` that was <u>assigned globally</u>.

The second `print()` shows that the <u>global test</u> has been <u>changed</u> by the function from 25 to 220.

Using global variables is generally bad practice

1) When you use `global` it <u>overrides</u> Python <u>automatically</u> giving objects a <u>scope</u>, so it should only be used <u>when necessary</u>. Forcing you to <u>add another line</u> is Python's way of telling you that this shouldn't become your <u>standard habit</u>.
2) Using <u>global variables</u> unnecessarily can cause <u>problems</u> in big programs — it can be hard to <u>keep track</u> of the <u>value</u> of <u>variables</u> as this depends on what <u>functions</u> are <u>called</u> and in what <u>order</u>.

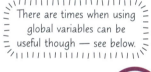

There are times when using global variables can be useful though — see below.

In big projects programmers can work on their subroutines independently. Using global variables would make it difficult to test individual functions and would require programmers to keep track of the variable names their colleagues are using to avoid unintended consequences.

Constants shouldn't be modified

1) In general programming, <u>constants</u> are like variables but their values <u>can't change</u> after <u>initialisation</u>.
2) Python doesn't have <u>constants</u>, but you can <u>mimic</u> them by <u>capitalising variable names</u> and keeping them <u>global</u>.

EXAMPLE Part of an exchange rate program that uses global variables acting as program-wide constants.

<u>Constants</u> are often set at the top of a program — even <u>above function definitions</u>.

Setting named constants at the top means they can be updated once (e.g. when the exchange rate changes) and that'll apply to the whole program.

```
GBUS = 1.4
GBEU = 1.2
def to_dollars():
    dollars = pounds * GBUS
    print(dollars)
def to_euros():
    euros = pounds * GBEU
    print(euros)
```

<u>Setting constants</u> in the main program means that all of the <u>subroutines</u> are able to <u>access them</u> since they're <u>global</u>.

GBUS and GBEU are not true constants as they can be changed. It's normal to capitalise them and this helps reduce the risk of them being changed by mistake.

"Hear ye! Hear ye! I declare this variable global…"

A handy way of remembering the basic difference between global and local variables is that global variables are outside a function and local variables are inside a function. With practice it'll sink in and you'll be a pro.

Section Seven — Subroutines

Parameters and Return Values

Learning Objectives: This page has all the information you need to know about parameters, return values and how they interact with functions. You might say it's a very *functional* page...
- Understand the meaning of the terms parameter, argument and return value.
- Be able to use parameters and return values instead of global variables.

Parameters are put inside brackets in calling statements

1) Parameters are used to input data to a subroutine and return values from a subroutine.
2) Some built-in subroutines work with no parameters — for example, `.sort()` can have empty brackets. Others require one or more parameter, e.g. `sorted()` requires an object within the brackets to be a parameter.
3) Also, some subroutines return values and some don't — for example, `.sort()` (see p.65) doesn't as it directly changes the object but `sorted()` does as it gives you a list back.

A return value is any data that can be taken from a subroutine and then used within the main program.

You should be programming to subroutine interfaces

1) Well-designed subroutines are like a 'black box' — to use them, you shouldn't really need to know how they work, just what they do.
2) The interface of a subroutine defines the parameters it accepts and the return values it gives back at the end — e.g. a function called `abs()`.
3) `abs()` returns the positive version of a negative number (its absolute value) or just the number if it's positive. There are a few ways to do this — but it doesn't matter what `abs()` uses as it's like a black box.

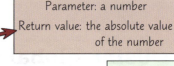

Use parameters and return values to avoid global variables

1) Using global variables means the subroutine is no longer a black box as you need to understand how it works in case it affects other parts of the program.
2) Instead of global variables, when defining your own functions you should:
   - Include parameter(s) when wanting to use data from the main program.
   - Include return value(s) when wanting to use data from the function back in the main program.

You can have multiple parameters but only one `return`. To return multiple values, use a data structure.

EXAMPLE Here are some examples of using parameters and return values to avoid global variables.

Parameters are variables that go inside the definition brackets (separated by commas).

```
def average(num1,num2,num3):
    total = num1 + num2 + num3
    print(total / 3)
average(10,15,20)
```
```
15.0
```

When `average()` is called, num1 is replaced by the value 10, num2 with 15 and num3 with 20.

Sometimes the actual values passed in (to give data to a subroutine) are called arguments. E.g. 10, 15, 20 are arguments here, whereas num1, num2, num3 are the parameters.

```
01  def rectangle_area(w,l):
02      area = w * l
03      return area
04  width = float(input("Enter a width: "))
05  length = float(input("Enter a length: "))
06  print("The area is", rectangle_area(width,length))
```

This function contains the local variables w, l and area. w and l are also parameters.

```
Enter a width: 5
Enter a length: 6
The area is 30.0
```

As line 3 uses `return`, the area value passed out from within the function can be used in a `print()` in the main program.

Using `return` instead of printing makes your subroutines more versatile. The value printed from within `average()` can't be used by the main program, but the value returned by `rectangle_area()` could be.

3) The `return` statement causes the function to end and go back to the calling statement — no other function code should come directly after it.

Practice Questions and Activities

Q1 Describe the difference between a global variable and a local variable.

....

....

....

Q2 Explain why each of these programs will result in an error.

a)
```
def volume():
    v = 200
print(v)
```
....

....

b)
```
w = 50
def volume():
    w = w / 5
    return w
volume()
print(w)
```
....

....

....

....

Q3 Have a look at the code below.

a) Circle the parameters, arguments and return value in the code. Then draw a line from each one to the relevant term.

b) Complete the output of the code.

```
def volume(w,l,h):
    v = w * l * h
    return v

print(volume(2,2,4))
```

Parameters

Arguments

Return value

Q4 Describe the purpose of a parameter in a function.

....

....

Q5 Write a program that calculates the area of a triangle.

- You should define a function called 'triangle'.
- The function should have two parameters h (height) and b (base).
- A calculation is carried out using these two variables to calculate the area.
- The area is returned to the main program.
- Call the function using values of your choice and output the result.

Modules

Learning Objectives
Some real-life objects are modular — they're made of similar units (modules) that are slightly different but together do a job. Python also uses modules to do particular tasks.

- Understand the purpose of modules.
- Learn about creating your own modules.
- Learn about the functionality of the math module.

There are lots of real-world examples of modules. Think about a digital camera where you can swap lenses, add an external flash or a memory card — all of these do a specific task but can be added or removed as required.

Modules contain lots of additional subroutines

1) A module is an external file that can act as a code library. In programming, these are where additional subroutines written by others can be imported into your program.
2) Python has some built-in modules that are installed with the main Python program.
3) The official Python website has a regularly updated list of available modules from independent developers. These modules can be used for many different purposes — from scientific and mathematical applications to providing subroutines to build graphical interfaces.
4) Modules save you time as you can use code that has already been written and tested.

You can import your own files as modules in Python

1) You can import another Python file into your program as a module as long as they're within the same folder. E.g. you might import your own file that contains global constants or subroutine definitions.
2) However, the rest of this section will focus on a few useful built-in modules that Python has to offer.

Some other modules might need to be manually installed using a command line tool like 'pip'.

The math module contains a range of mathematical tools

EXAMPLE Here are four useful tools that exist within the math module — but there are lots more.

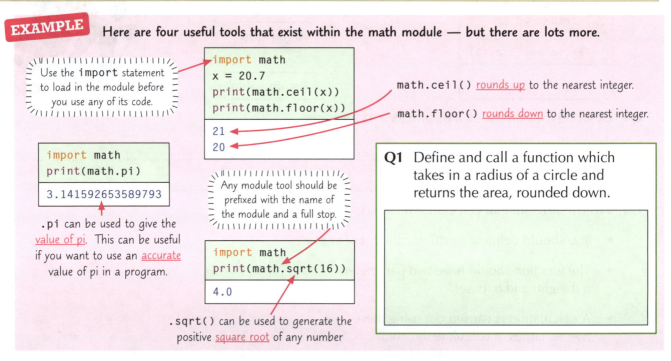

Use the `import` statement to load in the module before you use any of its code.

```
import math
x = 20.7
print(math.ceil(x))
print(math.floor(x))

21
20
```

`math.ceil()` rounds up to the nearest integer.

`math.floor()` rounds down to the nearest integer.

```
import math
print(math.pi)

3.141592653589793
```

`.pi` can be used to give the value of pi. This can be useful if you want to use an accurate value of pi in a program.

Any module tool should be prefixed with the name of the module and a full stop.

```
import math
print(math.sqrt(16))

4.0
```

`.sqrt()` can be used to generate the positive square root of any number

Q1 Define and call a function which takes in a radius of a circle and returns the area, rounded down.

What's the official animal of International Pi-day? The pi-thon...

Programming doesn't always have to be about finding solutions to problems — you can also code just for fun. You can even download joke modules, such as the `pyjokes` module, to have a go at creating something funny.

Section Seven — Subroutines

The Time Module

> **Learning Objectives**
>
> Programming with time is tricky as minutes, hours, days and weeks don't follow entirely logical sequences — 24 hours, 31 days... The time module makes all this easier to do.
> - Understand the purpose of the time module.
> - Learn about the functionality it offers.
> - Be able to use the time module in simple programs.

The time module can be used to time your programs

1) The .time() method from the time module gives you the number of seconds since the epoch — the epoch is a date used by computers as a reference point.
2) The value given by .time() isn't that useful on its own, but it can be used to see how long your program takes to run between two points.

The most commonly used epoch is January 1, 1970.

EXAMPLE This example uses the time module to calculate how long a program takes to run between two points.

Lines 3 and 7 are for getting the number of seconds since the epoch at both the start and end.

```
01  import time
02
03  startTime = time.time()
04
05  for i in range(1000000000): pass
06
07  endTime = time.time()
08  print("The time elapsed was",round(endTime - startTime,2),"seconds")
```
```
The time elapsed was 47.27 seconds
```

The second argument in round() is how many decimal places to round to.

After the end point, you can then subtract the two times to see how long it took.

Line 5 is dummy code used just to take up time (pass does nothing).

The time module can output the current date and time

1) Sometimes, you might need to show the current date and time — this might be part of a larger program, a login or booking system.
2) The local time can be displayed using the ctime method.

```
import time
localTime = time.ctime()
print(localTime)
```
```
Fri Mar 18 13:35:40 2022
```

Local time is the time wherever you are in the world — it's the same as your computer's clock.

Adding a delay can improve the user's experience

There are times when adding a short delay on screen gives the illusion of thinking time and gives the user time to keep up with what's happening. The sleep method adds a pause in seconds to any program.

```
import time
n1 = int(input("Type in any big number:"))
n2 = int(input("and another one to add to it:"))
print("These add up to....")
time.sleep(3)
print(n1 + n2)
```
```
Type in any big number:1500
and another one to add to it:7500
These add up to....
9000
```

Q1 Create a short question and answer program but add natural pauses into the responses using time.sleep().

Which animal always knows the time? A watch dog...

I know, I'm sorry... Anyway, using the time module is a great way of giving the user time to process what the program is doing. It can be tricky to follow code that just whizzes through everything.

Section Seven — Subroutines

The Random Module

Learning Objectives

Being random is difficult for a computer as they work using order and logical sequences. The random module has tools to help provide some random choices.

- Understand the purpose of the random module.
- Learn about the functionality it offers.
- Be able to create simple programs using the random module.

The random module isn't completely random

1) Python contains a random module but the numbers it generates are pseudorandom — this means the numbers it produces could be reproduced and therefore aren't truly random.
2) The numbers are calculated using the current system time, which is constantly changing.
3) However, these numbers are random enough for basic programming purposes.
4) `random.randint()` generates a random integer within a specified inclusive range.

```
import random
choice = random.randint(1,49)
print(choice)
```
```
22
```

The values can also include negative whole numbers.

An integer between 1 and 49 (inclusive) is generated at random.

Q1 Edit the program shown to generate a random number between -10 and 10. Don't include -10 and 10.

Random numbers can link to random responses

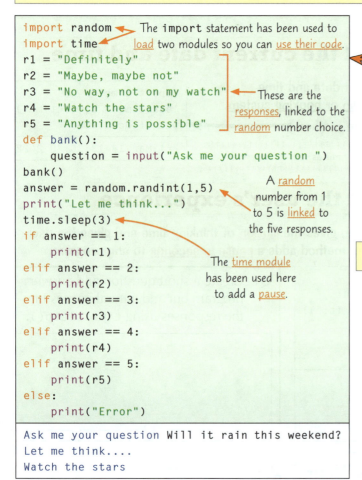

```
import random
import time
r1 = "Definitely"
r2 = "Maybe, maybe not"
r3 = "No way, not on my watch"
r4 = "Watch the stars"
r5 = "Anything is possible"
def bank():
    question = input("Ask me your question ")
bank()
answer = random.randint(1,5)
print("Let me think...")
time.sleep(3)
if answer == 1:
    print(r1)
elif answer == 2:
    print(r2)
elif answer == 3:
    print(r3)
elif answer == 4:
    print(r4)
elif answer == 5:
    print(r5)
else:
    print("Error")
```
```
Ask me your question Will it rain this weekend?
Let me think....
Watch the stars
```

The `import` statement has been used to load two modules so you can use their code.

These are the responses, linked to the random number choice.

A random number from 1 to 5 is linked to the five responses.

The time module has been used here to add a pause.

1) By linking a response to a randomly chosen number, a simple chatbot can be created.
2) This example is a version of a fortune telling game that provides an answer to any question.

Q2 Download the code on the left and edit it by doing the following:
- Add three more responses.
- Make the chatbot ask for another question after the first response.

You can repeat a random number

Rather than using the system time, a random number can also be generated from a specific value (the seed). If that same code is rerun, the same sequence of random numbers will be created.

```
import random
random.seed(10)
print(random.randint(1,50))
print(random.randint(1,50))
```
```
37
3
```

Try this program — you should get the same 'random' numbers.

Section Seven — Subroutines

Turtle Graphics

Learning Objectives

Python is capable of more than running calculations, dealing with time and asking questions. It can also draw. Here's a couple of pages on how to be artistic with Python.

- Understand the purpose of the turtle module.
- Learn about the graphical tools it offers and the shapes it can create.
- Be able to create a range of simple graphics.

Turtle is based on the floor turtle robots used in schools

1) Early floor robots, or turtles, allowed students to control the movement of a robot using basic programming commands — e.g. 'Go forward 10 paces, turn 90 degrees...'.
2) A pen could be added and the floor turtle could draw patterns on large pieces of paper.
3) The `turtle` module in Python uses the same basic idea but allows patterns to be drawn on-screen.

Turtle allows you to control a virtual pen

The 'pen' is placed in the centre of the screen and controlled with simple commands.

EXAMPLE Here's a simple square drawn with `Turtle`.

This moves the pen forward 50 pixels.

This turns the pen right 90 degrees.

At the start of every new turtle program, the turtle is facing to the right.

```
from turtle import *

pensize(2.5)
fd(50)
rt(90)
fd(50)
rt(90)
fd(50)
rt(90)
fd(50)
```

This is called the drawing arrow. It shows which way the turtle is facing.

The output is drawn in a new window.

`from turtle import *` is used here to get all of the `turtle` methods while avoiding needing to write the module name before them (like we did for `math`, `time`, and `random`).

Turtle commands are based around distance and angles

The table below covers the basic commands needed to create a range of simple and complex shapes.

`fd` = forward, `bk` = backward, `rt` = right and `lt` = left

Command	Description
fd(50)	Forward 50 pixels
bk(50)	Backward 50 pixels
rt(45)	Turn right 45 degrees
lt(45)	Turn left 45 degrees
circle(75)	Draw a circle with a radius of 75 pixels
penup()	Lift the pen (pen always starts down)
pendown()	Lower the pen
pensize(100)	Sets the pen size at 100 pixels
pencolor("red")	Sets the colour to red (note the spelling of 'color')
fillcolor("red")	Sets the fill colour of a shape.
begin_fill()	Stated before a shape is created.
end_fill()	Stated after a shape is created.
goto(x,y)	Moves the turtle to an absolute position on screen.

```
from turtle import *

pencolor("blue")
pensize(5)
fd(100)
rt(90)
fd(20)
rt(90)
fd(80)
lt(90)
fd(60)
lt(90)
fd(80)
rt(90)
fd(20)
rt(90)
fd(100)
rt(90)
fd(100)
```

This 'C' is the output of the code on the left.

Q1 Use the commands discussed so far to draw one or more letters of your name in Python.

Section Seven — Subroutines

Turtle Graphics

Repeating commands is more efficient

The square example on the previous page repeats the same pair of commands (draw a line 50 pixels long and then turn 90 degrees) four times.

EXAMPLE A square has been drawn using fewer lines of code than on the previous page by using a `for` loop.

The pen moves forward and turns right four times.

```
from turtle import *
pencolor("green")
pensize(5)
for i in range(4):
    fd(100)
    rt(90)
```

Changing the number in brackets after `pensize` will change the thickness of the line (or lines) being output. The higher the number, the thicker the line and vice versa.

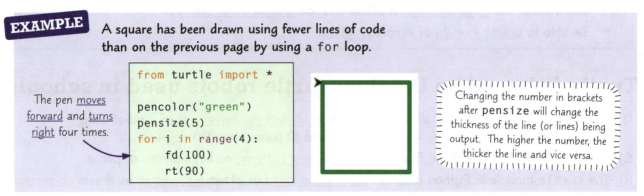

Combining techniques creates more complex drawings

The three examples below combine the techniques used so far to create three different shapes.

EXAMPLE The code below has been used to create a blue triangle.

```
from turtle import *
fillcolor("blue")
begin_fill()
for t in range(3):
    fd(150)
    lt(120)
end_fill()
```

Any shape can be filled by setting the `fillcolor()` and then adding the opening and closing statements `begin_fill()` and `end_fill()` around it.

The line and angle are repeated three times to create a triangle.

Don't forget to use the American spelling of 'color'.

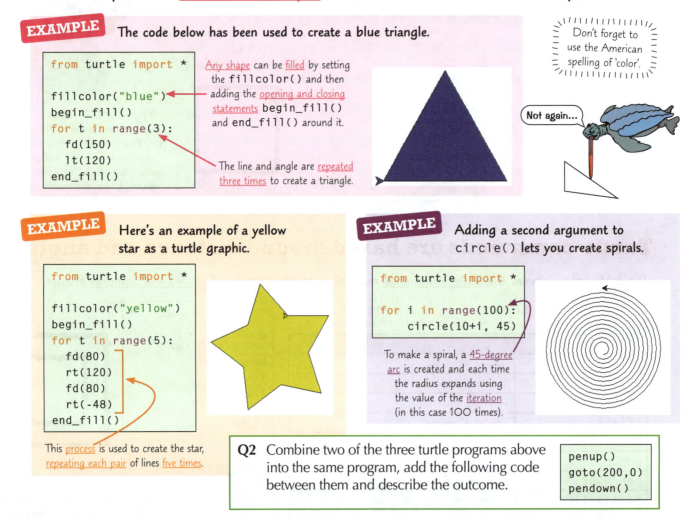

EXAMPLE Here's an example of a yellow star as a turtle graphic.

```
from turtle import *
fillcolor("yellow")
begin_fill()
for t in range(5):
    fd(80)
    rt(120)
    fd(80)
    rt(-48)
end_fill()
```

This process is used to create the star, repeating each pair of lines five times.

EXAMPLE Adding a second argument to `circle()` lets you create spirals.

```
from turtle import *
for i in range(100):
    circle(10+i, 45)
```

To make a spiral, a 45-degree arc is created and each time the radius expands using the value of the iteration (in this case 100 times).

Q2 Combine two of the three turtle programs above into the same program, add the following code between them and describe the outcome.

```
penup()
goto(200,0)
pendown()
```

It's time to get out of your shell and have some fun with turtle...

You can do more than make shapes and spirals with `turtle`. The possibilities are almost endless. Play around with pen styles, different angles and colours to see just how creative you can be with turtle graphics.

Section Seven — Subroutines

Practice Questions and Activities

Q1 List three modules and describe their purpose.

1 ....

2 ....

3 ....

Q2 In programming, what is the date 1st January 1970 considered to be?

....

Q3 Describe the output created by this program.

```
import time
localTime = time.ctime()
print(localTime)
```

Q4 Write a short program that will generate a random number between two numbers given by the user.

Q5 Use `turtle` to write programs that create the following:

a) A triangle with a red fill   b) A capital 'T' with a green fill   c) A hexagon with a yellow outline

You can use these output boxes to sketch out each shape as you go. It's important to keep in mind the orientation of your turtle after each movement.

Section Seven — Subroutines

Coding Challenges for Section Seven

There's a lot to take in from Section Seven. The challenges below will help you see what you know and what you're less confident on. Once you're ready, head to the link on the contents page to get those Python programs.

Challenge 1

You've been asked to create a small programming game that challenges the user to stop the program after 10 seconds have passed. The user has to count the 10 seconds in their head.

It should meet the following criteria:
- The user presses 'enter' to start the clock.
- The user presses 'enter' to stop the clock.
- The time between the two inputs is displayed to two decimal places.

Challenge 2

A film review website has asked you to create a simple chatbot that will appear occasionally to chat to the user.

The program should:
- Ask the user about one of five random films. The films can be five of your own choice.
- Ask the user to give it a star rating out of four.
- Depending on the rating given it will give one of the following responses:
    1) 1 star: "Sorry to hear that."
    2) 2 stars: "Sounds like it was OK then."
    3) 3 stars: "Great to hear, I'll check it out myself."
    4) 4 stars: "I thought so too, I bet you can't wait to see it again!"
- Time delays should be used to improve the user's experience.
- Any other features you feel suitable can be added.

Challenge 3

A messaging app is being built using Python and you've been asked to create a sample emoji using the turtle module.

The emoji should:
- look happy
- include at least two eyes and a mouth.

You'll need to make sure you lift the pen when creating multiple shapes.

Challenge 4

An online fan club generates an automated username and password when creating an account. You have been asked to write part of the program.

The program should make use of user-defined functions to do the following:
- Ask the user for their first and last name.
- Use a function to create a username of the first letter of their first name and the last three letters of their last name.
- For the password, generate a sequence of random letters (upper and lower case), numbers and symbols that's 10 characters in length. Ensure that there are no repeated characters in the password — e.g. 'aa', '22' or '!!'. Letters should be twice as likely to occur as numbers or symbols. Numbers and symbols should be equally likely.

Section Eight — File Handling

Using External Files

Learning Objectives

All the data used in your programs so far has been written directly into the source code in a .py file. However, it's often helpful to use data from other files in your programs.

- Understand why external files are often used.
- Understand the distinction between a text and a binary file.

Values are held in the volatile main memory

1) The programs you've made so far have contained a lot of data being held in variables and data structures.
2) These values will be held in your computer's main memory — in most cases the largest component of this is random access memory (RAM).
3) RAM is volatile memory — this means that all data held in it is lost when the computer is turned off.
4) Not only are the values you have in your Python programs not held if the computer shuts down, but when the program ends, the computer frees up the main memory. This deletes any values you had held.
5) You can see this in action using the Shell.

Ever suddenly lost power while working on something important and it didn't save? This is why.

```
>>> variable = "This value is held in main memory."
>>> print(variable)
This value is held in main memory
```

```
>>> # Closing and then opening a new Shell
>>> print(variable)
NameError: name 'variable' is not defined
```

When a new Shell is opened, the previous value held for `variable` has already been lost.

Data is stored on the secondary storage

1) For storing data more permanently, instead of just temporarily holding it within your program, it should be saved to an external file. These will be held on the computer's non-volatile storage device — usually a HDD (hard disk drive) or a SSD (solid state drive).
2) Almost every program you use relies on being able to open, read from, edit and save to other files — it's what makes these programs useful in many cases.

REAL WORLD CODE

Almost all video games use external files to save progress within the game. Loading or saving these files can take a while as secondary storage is much slower than main memory.

All files are stored in binary

1) Thankfully it's not something programmers need to think about too often, but behind the scenes everything is represented in the 0s and 1s of binary.
2) The different types of files and file extensions that'll be on your computer all represent the data in binary in different ways.
3) We'll focus on simple files which store human readable characters — these are what we call text files. They're still stored in binary, but Python is able to convert to text for you.
4) A file without much or any text (a binary file) is trickier to use since there won't be this automatic conversion — you'll need to deal with the raw binary yourself. We won't touch these here, but down the road you may deal with binary files without any text content like audio or image files.

By default, Python converts to and from binary text data using the character set Unicode (an extension of ASCII).

My memory is so volatile these days... Right, back to Cobra.

Remember to save your work regularly. Python can't run without being saved but you don't want to have written 3 hours worth of code and then, boom, the power goes and all your work disappears... Sigh...

Reading from Text Files

Learning Objectives

There are 4 basic operations you can do to external files: create, read, update and delete them. We're going to look at these CRUD operations one by one, but starting with the chunkiest one — the reading.

- To be able to read in data from a text file.
- To be able to parse data from a text file into a list.

Text files come in a few forms but they're all plain

1) A text file is any file that Python is able to read and convert to printable text.
2) To be able to do this without a hitch, you need to be using very simple file formats — for this section we're just going to use .txt files and .csv files.
3) These files store plain text only, meaning there is no formatting. When text is saved with formatting like varying colours, different fonts, and bolding from a word processor, this requires additional data to be saved alongside the text.
4) This may mean Python cannot convert it to strings — which is why you should avoid using other file formats unless you fancy doing a lot more manual work.

Plain text .txt and .csv files can be created and viewed in simple text editors like Notepad or TextEdit. Avoid opening them with word processors.

To get data from a file you need to open it in read mode

EXAMPLE Reading a text file called 'hamlet.txt' to output Prince Hamlet's famous monologue to the user.

```
print("Hamlet: Act 3, Scene 1.")

myFile = open("hamlet.txt","r")

for line in myFile:
    print(line)

myFile.close()
```

Hamlet: Act 3, Scene 1.
To be, or not to be: that is the question:

Whether 'tis nobler in the mind to suffer

The slings and arrows of outrageous fortune,

Or to take arms against a sea of troubles,

This is just a snippet of the full output. If we included the whole hamlet.txt, this book would just be Hamlet...

hamlet.txt
To be, or not to be: that is the question:
Whether 'tis nobler in the mind to suffer
The slings and arrows of outrageous fortune,
Or to take arms against a sea of troubles,

This box shows a small part of the text file. You'll see more of these later in the section.

This opens the text file and assigns the file object to the variable myFile. The first argument is the file's name — for now, this must be in the same folder as the .py file. The second argument is the mode — when reading, type r.

You can now loop through the whole file, line by line, using a for loop. In this example we're just printing the contents of each line.

.close() terminates the connection to the external file. Do this as soon as you're done with the reading steps — this is not necessarily right at the end of your program.

The output has a blank line between each line of the file — this is because in the original text file there's a hidden \n at the end of each line which is also printed.

To close, or not to close?

1) Once you're done using the file, it's good practice to apply the .close() method. This prevents you from accidentally using that file object afterwards — you'd get an error if you tried to print() a line after the file is closed.

2) Don't panic if you forget .close() when reading from a file — when the program ends Python will mop it up for you. Leaving it open unnecessarily though does result in some risk of corruption and can mean lines aren't properly written to it (p.85).

Section Eight — File Handling

Reading from Text Files

Use file object methods to read with more control

The `for` loop in the example on the previous page does a lot of work for you — but sometimes you might want to go through the lines of text separately. There are 2 key methods that help with this.

EXAMPLE The `.readline()` method keeps track of where you are in the file, giving you the next line each time it's called.

Using `.readlines()` is useful if you want to pinpoint a specific line.

```
myFile = open("hamlet.txt","r")

# Print the first two lines
print(myFile.readline())
print(myFile.readline())

myFile.close()

To be, or not to be: that is the question:

Whether 'tis nobler in the mind to suffer
```

```
myFile = open("hamlet.txt","r")

# Store each line as an item in a list
contents = myFile.readlines()
print(contents[0])
print(contents[1])

myFile.close()

To be, or not to be: that is the question:

Whether 'tis nobler in the mind to suffer
```

Use `.read()` if you want the whole file as a string. Add arguments to these methods if you want to limit their size — e.g. `read(5)` gives the next 5 characters.

Again, the extra line breaks are caused by the \n characters hidden in the file — see below for how to remove these.

CSV files add much more structure

There's not a lot more we can do with the Hamlet text file, as it isn't structured. Many text files that contain information useful to us will have data structured into records and fields, as .csv files do. These files are often used to store data that could be represented in table form.

EXAMPLE CSV stands for comma-separated values and that's how the files are structured.

A record is a line, or row, in the file — here there are 4 records, one for each play being stored.

plays.csv
Hamlet,1602,30557
Othello,1604,26450
Tempest,1611,16633
Macbeth,1606,17121

A field is like a column in a table. In CSV files, the values in each field have commas to separate them. The comma is called the delimiter.

Play	Year Completed	Word count
Hamlet	1602	30557
Othello	1604	26450
Tempest	1611	16633
Macbeth	1606	17121

Parsing a file means reading it and then organising it

EXAMPLE Read the 'plays.csv' file and make a 2D list so individual values can be easily used later on.

This initialises the list `plays` that will be used to hold the parsed content of the file.

A `with` statement is an alternative to having separate `open()` and `.close()` lines. The benefit of `with` is that the file is closed automatically when its indentation ends.

To get every line, a `for` loop can be used.

```
plays = []
with open("plays.csv","r") as myFile:
    for line in myFile:
        line = line.strip()
        record = line.split(",")
        plays.append(record)
print("The parsed 2D list:", plays)
print("The second play stored:", plays[1][0])
```

```
The parsed 2D list: [['Hamlet', '1602',
'30557'], ['Othello', '1604', '26450'],
['Tempest', '1611', '16633'], ['Macbeth',
'1606', '17121']]
The second play stored: Othello
```

`.strip()` removes any unnecessary characters, like spaces, at the start and end of the line — this includes the pesky hidden \n character.

`.split()` will break apart the line whenever it sees a comma, or whatever the delimiter argument is, and return a list with the separated values as items. Once this is done it can be added to the `plays` list.

You can now access each individual field in each record.

Section Eight — File Handling

Managing External Files

Learning Objectives

In this section so far, we've assumed that your text file is sat happily in the same folder as your program code. It's not always that simple though, so it's time to consider general file management.

- Understand the difference between absolute and relative file paths and why relative paths are preferred.
- To be able to use methods from the OS module.

To read files you need to tell Python where they are

1) Before you get on with creating, writing, and deleting files — take a minute to consider where files are located.
2) Secondary storage is organised into folders. These are also sometimes called directories. Here's part of the directory structure.
3) When you used `open("plays.csv","r")` on the previous page, the program was able to read it as that text file is in the same folder as the Python file used.
4) If you tried to open `othello.txt` in the same way, you'd get an error since it's not in the same folder as the .py file. Python won't go out of its way to look for it anywhere else.

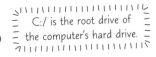

```
file = open("othello.txt","r")
```
```
FileNotFoundError: [Errno 2] No such file or directory: 'othello.txt'
```

5) Instead, the full file path could be supplied to tell the program exactly where to look. Including all folders like this is what's called an absolute path.

```
file = open("C:/Users/CGP/Python Work/Text Files/othello.txt","r")
```

C:/ is the root drive of the computer's hard drive.

6) The problem is that this absolute path is specific to your computer, which is not ideal if you want to give your program to anyone else. They'd get the `FileNotFoundError` when they run the code.
7) It's often best to use relative paths instead — these just say where the external file is compared to where the program file is.

```
file = open("./Text Files/othello.txt","r")
```

8) In relative paths, one full stop is used to mean this current folder, and two full stops are used to mean the folder above the one you're currently in, so to access `macbeth.txt` the relative path is this.

```
file = open("../macbeth.txt","r")
```

The OS module has file and folder management methods

1) Dealing with external files can be a bit fiddly. Any small mistake or inconsistency in the file path will result in an error. Each operating system (OS) manages files in subtly different ways too.
2) To check to see if a file or folder exists before you try and open it, you can use the OS module — which has lots of tools, like the ones below, to help you deal with files and OSs.

```
import os
if os.path.isfile("./Text Files/tempest.txt"):
    print("This file exists.")
else:
    print("This file doesn't exist.")
```
```
This file doesn't exist.
```

This can be used to check if a file exists. If it doesn't, you could then create it.

.remove() deletes any file you ask it to permanently so take extreme care when using it.

```
import os
# Create a folder:
os.mkdir("./CSV files")
# Delete a file:
os.remove("plays.csv")
# All files/folders at a path as a list:
print(os.listdir("."))
```
```
['CSV files', 'file handling.py',
'hamlet.txt', 'Text Files']
```

Section Eight — File Handling

Writing to Text Files

Learning Objectives

To save data from your program you'll want to write to files. This is pretty simple, but getting the data in the correct format can take a bit of trial and error.

- To be able to write to an external text file.
- To understand the difference between write and append mode.

To add data to an external file use .write()

EXAMPLE Writing information about jobs at a software development company to an external .csv file.

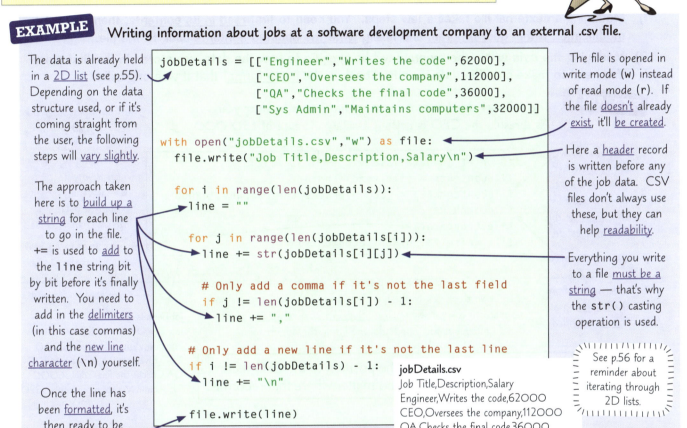

The data is already held in a 2D list (see p.55). Depending on the data structure used, or if it's coming straight from the user, the following steps will vary slightly.

The approach taken here is to build up a string for each line to go in the file. += is used to add to the line string bit by bit before it's finally written. You need to add in the delimiters (in this case commas) and the new line character (\n) yourself.

Once the line has been formatted, it's then ready to be written to the file.

The file is opened in write mode (w) instead of read mode (r). If the file doesn't already exist, it'll be created.

Here a header record is written before any of the job data. CSV files don't always use these, but they can help readability.

Everything you write to a file must be a string — that's why the str() casting operation is used.

See p.56 for a reminder about iterating through 2D lists.

The code creates this CSV file.

```
jobDetails.csv
Job Title,Description,Salary
Engineer,Writes the code,62000
CEO,Oversees the company,112000
QA,Checks the final code,36000
Sys Admin,Maintains computers,32000
```

Open in w mode to overwrite and use a to write at the end

1) Opening in write (w) mode will create a file if one doesn't exist — but if one does exist, it'll delete anything there already.
2) To add more details to the end of a file, use append (a) mode.

```
with open("jobDetails.csv","a") as file:
    file.write("\nDesigner,Determines the UI,45000")
```

This only shows part of jobDetails.csv plus the new line.

```
Sys Admin,Maintains computers,32000
Designer,Determines the UI,45000
```

Writing isn't always straightforward

Here are two common logic errors within one bit of harmless looking code.

```
textFile = open("example.txt","w")
textFile.write("My first line.")
textFile.write("My second line.")
```

Error 1: You might run this code, open the text file and see nothing. This is because the text is not always actually written until you .close() it. Remember, with does this for you.

Error 2: Even if it does save, it would look like this. To fix, make sure you add in the \n.

example.txt
My first line.My second line.

Check that the text files aren't open in another program when you run the code — this might also prevent them being written to.

Section Eight — File Handling

Updating and Deleting Content in Text Files

Learning Objectives

As file handling involves going through the OS, there aren't any magic Python methods to modify files easily — it requires a bit of manual work.

- Understand the steps involved in modifying content within a text file.
- To be able to update or delete data held in a text file.

You're unlikely to get code working perfectly on the first try — back up any important files in case you accidentally lose data.

Updating a value in a text file

1) Modifying an external file takes a few steps. You need to first read in its contents, then make the modification within your program and finally write the updated contents back to the file.
2) Modifying the data within the program will be specific to how the data was stored in the first place. You need to make sure the data is written back in the same format that it was originally.

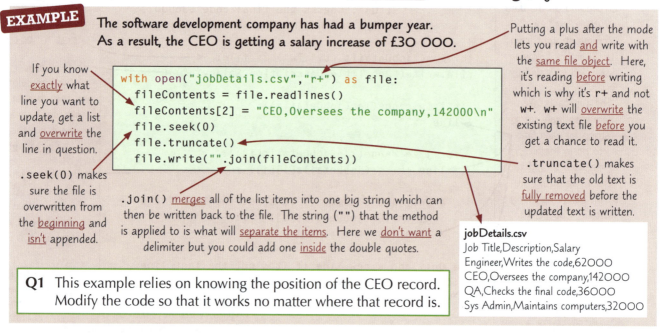

EXAMPLE

The software development company has had a bumper year. As a result, the CEO is getting a salary increase of £30 000.

```
with open("jobDetails.csv","r+") as file:
    fileContents = file.readlines()
    fileContents[2] = "CEO,Oversees the company,142000\n"
    file.seek(0)
    file.truncate()
    file.write("".join(fileContents))
```

If you know exactly what line you want to update, get a list and overwrite the line in question.

.seek(0) makes sure the file is overwritten from the beginning and isn't appended.

.join() merges all of the list items into one big string which can then be written back to the file. The string ("") that the method is applied to is what will separate the items. Here we don't want a delimiter but you could add one inside the double quotes.

Putting a plus after the mode lets you read and write with the same file object. Here, it's reading before writing which is why it's r+ and not w+. w+ will overwrite the existing text file before you get a chance to read it.

.truncate() makes sure that the old text is fully removed before the updated text is written.

jobDetails.csv
Job Title,Description,Salary
Engineer,Writes the code,62000
CEO,Oversees the company,142000
QA,Checks the final code,36000
Sys Admin,Maintains computers,32000

Q1 This example relies on knowing the position of the CEO record. Modify the code so that it works no matter where that record is.

Deleting a value is much the same

When it comes to file handling there are a lot of different ways you can do it. The example below shows an alternative approach to the one above, but this time for deleting a field in a record.

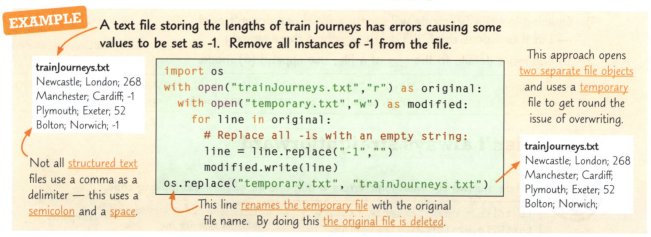

EXAMPLE

A text file storing the lengths of train journeys has errors causing some values to be set as -1. Remove all instances of -1 from the file.

trainJourneys.txt
Newcastle; London; 268
Manchester; Cardiff; -1
Plymouth; Exeter; 52
Bolton; Norwich; -1

```
import os
with open("trainJourneys.txt","r") as original:
    with open("temporary.txt","w") as modified:
        for line in original:
            # Replace all -1s with an empty string:
            line = line.replace("-1","")
            modified.write(line)
os.replace("temporary.txt", "trainJourneys.txt")
```

Not all structured text files use a comma as a delimiter — this uses a semicolon and a space.

This line renames the temporary file with the original file name. By doing this the original file is deleted.

This approach opens two separate file objects and uses a temporary file to get round the issue of overwriting.

trainJourneys.txt
Newcastle; London; 268
Manchester; Cardiff;
Plymouth; Exeter; 52
Bolton; Norwich;

Sadly there's no magic wand to wave to change your text files...

File handling requires patience and some trial and error — don't worry if it takes a while to get your head around at first. It's always a good idea to back up your files before you start though to avoid coding rage.

Practice Questions and Activities

Q1 Explain why external files are commonly used with computer programs.

....

....

Q2 Describe what's happening in the program below.

```
01 import random
02
03 theFile = open("pythonFacts.txt", "r")
04 allFacts = theFile.readlines()
05
06 print("There are", len(allFacts), "facts stored.")
07 print("A fact is:", allFacts[random.randint(0, len(allFacts)-1)].strip())
08
09 theFile.close()
```

pythonFacts.txt
They are cold blooded reptiles
They like to live in warm and wet climates
All species are non-venomous
Many species are excellent swimmers

....

....

....

....

....

Q3 Look at the directory structure below. Assuming your source code is in the `countries analyser.py` file, state the relative paths of the following text files.

a) Europe.csv

....

b) Asia.csv

....

c) South America.txt

....

```
v 🖿 C
  v 🖿 Programming
    v 🖿 Other Files
      v 🖿 Data
        └ 📄 Asia.csv
      └ 📄 Europe.csv
    └ 📄 Africa.csv
    └ 📄 countries analyser.py
  └ 📄 South America.txt
```

Q4 Complete the gaps so that this program will add a timestamp (the current date and time) on a new line of the `usageLog.txt` file every time the program is executed.

    .... time

    with ....("usageLog.txt", "............") as ....:

        .... = ...ctime()

        file.write(timestamp .... "....................")

Q5 Outline the steps involved in updating or deleting items within an external text file.

....

....

....

Coding Challenges for Section Eight

For challenges 2 and 3, there are .txt files to download from the link on the contents page. This link will also have sample programs for each one of the challenges — have a go before you take a snoop at these though.

Challenge 1

Code a game of 'Higher or Lower' between the user and the program. Here's how the game works:

- The program generates a random number between 1 and 100 (inclusive)
- The user needs to guess the number that was generated. If they get it correct, the round ends.
- If the user guesses incorrectly, they're told Higher (if the guess was too low) or Lower (if the guess was too high).
- This process repeats until the user guesses correctly.

The user's score is then printed — this is how many guesses they made before they guessed correctly. If this is 6 or less, then the user wins. Otherwise, the program wins.

Head back to p.76 if you need a refresh on the random module.

To save progress after a round is finished, save the user's score to an external file. Each time the program starts, it should output the number of times the user and the computer have won.

Challenge 2

A Computing teacher has a text file that contains some questions about Computer Science — part of this file is shown on the right. Each question and answer is separated by a double hyphen.

```
CSQuestions&CorrectAnswers.txt
What is the decimal number 10 in 4 bit binary? -- 1010
What is the binary number 11 in decimal? -- 3
How many bits are there in a nibble? -- 4
What does ROM stand for? -- Read Only Memory
What is 13 MOD 3? -- 1
What does IP stand for? -- Internet Protocol
```

Your task is to make a quiz program for the teacher. The program should:

- Randomly select 5 questions to show to the user. This will be considered one quiz.
- Automatically mark each question and let the user know if they were correct or incorrect. If they are incorrect, show the correct answer. Make sure that mismatching capital letters don't result in a correct answer being marked as incorrect.
- Display a score at the end of the quiz. A correct answer gives 1 point.
- Add incorrect answers to another text file called 'WrongAnswers.csv' alongside the original question and the current time and date. This is to be used by the teacher at a later point to see if there are common questions students are getting wrong across multiple random quizzes.

Challenge 3

A text file contains the estimated populations for lots of different economies around the world — part of this file is shown here.

```
populationData.csv
Economy Name,Economy Code,Population
Aruba,ABW,106766
Bolivia,BOL,11673029
Jamaica,JAM,2961161
Korea, Rep.,KOR,51780579
Palau,PLW,18092
```

An added complication in this dataset is that some economy names have commas in.

Your program should do the following:

- Show the user the largest and smallest population currently recorded in the file. The average population size should also be shown for context.
- Then give the user the choice to do one of the following tasks:
  1) Allow the user to view only the economies with a population above a certain value they specify.
  2) Change the population size of an economy when the user enters the economy code and the new value. (The figures in this file are from 2020 so a user might want to update them.)

Section Nine — Making Programs Robust

Validation

Learning Objectives

Making programs that are user-ready is an important part of programming. Users are notoriously tricky customers, so you'll need to remain on guard...

- Understand what is meant by robustness.
- Understand the purpose of input validation.
- To be able to perform common validation checks.

Robust programs should handle common errors

1) Software that regularly encounters errors and crashes isn't robust. Robustness is the ability of your program to respond to unexpected events and handle them.
2) Encountering errors is a standard part of programming, but it's not acceptable to still have them in your programs when they're being used by actual users.

Validation can make your programs more robust

1) Validation is checking that data is valid. In other words, it's checking that the data within the program is what's expected and is usable.
2) Programs are written to deal with a particular type (or types) of input but user inputs into a program are often unpredictable and unexpected.
3) Since invalid data can cause errors, validation aids robustness and security.

Injection attacks are when an attacker tries to get the program to execute their malicious code by including it as a regular input. These attacks can be avoided by using input validation.

EXAMPLE Here are some instances where you're expecting a certain data input but what's received is different and causes an error.

```
age = int(input("Please enter your age: "))
print("Thank you")
```
```
Please enter your age: Forty Seven
ValueError: invalid literal for int() with base 10: 'Forty Seven'
```

int() requires it in the format 47, so Forty Seven isn't valid.

Here the user provides a valid integer, but it can't be used as there's no item at the index they specify (3).

```
numeros = ["Uno","Dos","Tres"]
index = int(input("Enter a position: "))
print(numeros[index])
```
```
Enter a position: 3
IndexError: list index out of range
```

This prompt isn't very helpful for the user. Using clear prompts can help avoid issues with data entry — it isn't always the user's fault.

Defensive programmers expect the unexpected

1) When deciding what validation to add to a program, you should think defensively. Defensive design involves considering how users might misuse a program and trying to prevent them doing this. Having this defensive mindset means you'll write and test your programs while anticipating user errors.
2) As a general rule, you should check your programs are robust by trying four types of test data:

Name	Description	Examples
Normal data	Data your program is able to work with.	14, 15, 16, 17, 18
Boundary (extreme) data	Data that's close to being erroneous — you may or may not think it's valid depending on the context.	13, 19
Invalid data	Data that's in the correct format but should be rejected by the program.	7, 350, 14539
Erroneous data	Data that your program isn't designed to work with and so might break it if you don't validate.	Hello, Huh?, +@!

Examples in this table are from a program that asks teenagers to enter their age.

Validation

Validation can check the type of data inputted

1) The ValueError on the previous page happened as the user didn't type in an integer as expected.
2) To add robustness, you can check the data type of the user input before doing something like casting it.
3) String methods like isdigit and isalpha return True if the string is just an integer or is made up of letters from the alphabet, respectively.

EXAMPLE Using .isdigit() and .isalpha() with a while loop to ensure valid data is entered.

Ask for your inputs — don't try and do anything to these until they're definitely valid.

A while loop is needed as you can't know how many times the user will get it wrong — it's indefinite.

```
firstName = input("What's your name? ")
age = input("What's your age? ")

while firstName.isalpha() == False or age.isdigit() == False:
    firstName = input("Reenter your name: ")
    age = input("Reenter your age: ")

age = int(age)
```

firstName should be completely alphabetical and age should just be an integer. If either one of these isn't true, ask the user to reenter.

```
What's your name? AJ!
What's your age? Sixteen
Reenter your name: AJ
Reenter your age: 16.2
Reenter your name: AJ
Reenter your age: 16
```

Both of these are invalid, so it loops.

AJ is fine, but age.isDigit() is false for 16.2 because of the decimal point.

These two inputs are valid, so the loop ends. You can then cast age to an integer.

There isn't a handy method for floats unfortunately — see p.95 for how to check those.

4) If you want to check the current data type of an object you can use the function isinstance. For example, this can be useful if you want to adapt your subroutine code depending on what arguments are supplied.

```
age = 27
check = isinstance(age, int)
print(check)
True
```

The first argument is what you're checking.

The second argument is the name of the data type to check — here it's an integer.

The second argument could also be a data structure, such as list, tuple or set.

Use len() for length checks

1) len() can be used to check the length of inputted data. For example, you can keep asking for a PIN until it has a length of 4.
2) A null or presence check sees if a value has actually been provided — in many cases this is really a check for length 0.

```
pinEntry = input("Please enter your new 4-digit PIN: ")
while len(pinEntry) != 4:
    pinEntry = input("Please try again: ")
print("New PIN accepted, thank you.")
```

```
Please enter your new 4-digit PIN: 12345
Please try again: 1234
New PIN accepted, thank you.
```

Use range checks to ensure only certain values are used

1) You can use relational operators to check that values fall within a range — e.g. 13 <= n <= 19 would evaluate to True if n is in the range 13 – 19 (inclusive).
2) You can also use the range function to generate a sequence to test.
3) In this example range(0,101,10) generates the sequence (0,10,20,...,100). The user input 'n' is accepted if it's in the sequence.

```
acceptable = range(0,101,10)
n = int(input("Please enter number: "))
if n in acceptable:
    print("Number accepted.")
else:
    print("Number not accepted.")
```

```
Please enter number: 62
Number not accepted.
```

62 isn't in the sequence so isn't accepted.

Regular Expressions

Learning Objectives

Regular expressions can be very advanced, but even knowing the basics can be useful for dealing with strings and performing validation.

- Understand the purpose of regular expressions when carrying out a string search.
- Understand the purpose of the `re` module.
- Learn about the functionality the `re` module offers.
- To be able to experiment with string searches and use special characters.
- Learn how regular expressions can be used to validate user data.

Don't be scared, this is my regular expression!

Regular expressions can be used to search a string

1) Regular expressions are patterns of characters — you can use a regular expression to search a string for a specific pattern.
2) Regular expressions can often be used in:
   - internet search engines
   - search tools for finding specific text in a text document or webpage
   - search tools for finding files in your operating system
3) Regular expressions are also used in online forms that check and validate details inputted by the user, such as a password.

Python has a built-in regular expression module

1) The regular expression module (`re`) can be imported in the same way as any other module, using `import re`.
2) Three useful methods it includes are:
   - `.findall()` — lists all matching characters or strings.
   - `.search()` — returns the first time a match appears.
   - `.sub()` — replaces a matching string with another.

The `re` module is often referred to as RegEx by programmers.

EXAMPLE Here are examples of the `findall()`, `search()` and `sub()` methods working with the `re` module.

```
import re
text = "A long time ago"
x = re.findall("o",text)
print(x)
```
```
['o', 'o']
```

Using `re.findall` will return all matching strings. In this case "o" in the variable `text`.

The character is found twice.

```
import re
text = "Welcome to the party!"
x = re.search("party",text)
print(x)
if x:
    print("You have a match")
else:
    print("No match")
```
```
<re.Match object; span=(15, 20), match='party'>
You have a match
```

`re.search()` returns a "match object" for the first match it finds.

If a match is found then x evaluates to true.

You can get the position of the match as a tuple using the `x.span()` method.

```
import re
text = "You dream, I dream,
we all dream for ice cream!"
x = re.sub("dream","scream",text)
print(x)
```
```
You scream, I scream, we all
scream for ice cream!
```

The string `dream` is replaced with `scream`.

Q1 Use the `re` module to output an 'i' for each time the letter appears in 'Mississippi'.

Section Nine — Making Programs Robust

Regular Expressions

Wildcards can be used if part of a string is unknown

1) So far the regular expressions have only looked for specific letter patterns, e.g. "o", "party" or "dream". But they can also include special characters called wildcards.
2) Wildcards can be used to stand in for unknown characters or indicate quantities of characters within regular expressions.
3) A full stop (.) is a wildcard that represents any character. In the example on the left, it's used to allow for different spellings (Isabel and Isobel would both be found).

```
import re
text = "Isobel looked up at the stars"
x = re.search("Is.bel",text)
if x:
    print("Match")
else:
    print("No match")
Match
```

To search for a full stop, you can escape with \ (add a \ before the .).

```
import re
text = "I'm getting too old for this!"
x = re.findall("[a-f]",text)
print(x)
['e', 'd', 'f']
```

A selection of characters within square brackets searches for any of the characters. For example, between a and f.

These letters match the search term so re.findall() returns a list of them.

Is.bel and [a-f] are treated as regular expressions and not just normal strings by the methods search and findall.

You can use regular expressions in validation

1) You can also use the .findall() and .search() methods to make your program more robust.
2) Regular expressions can be used to validate that user inputs follow specific patterns — this is known as a format check.

EXAMPLE Use regular expressions to make sure flight codes consist of two uppercase letters followed by a 1-4 digit number.

Two groups of characters are needed — capital letters and digits 0 to 9.

The ^ tells .search() to start looking at the beginning of the string and $ specifies the end (nothing should come after this in the string).

Like the validation examples before, a loop iterates while there isn't a match.

```
import re
flightCode = input("Enter flight code: ")
regex = "^[A-Z]{2}[0-9]{1,4}$"
match = re.search(regex,flightCode)

while not match:
    flightCode = input("Reenter flight code: ")
    match = re.search(regex,flightCode)
print("Success.")
```

```
Enter flight code: CGP99
Reenter flight code: 101
Reenter flight code: A1
Reenter flight code: yz22222
Reenter flight code: AB98
Success.
```

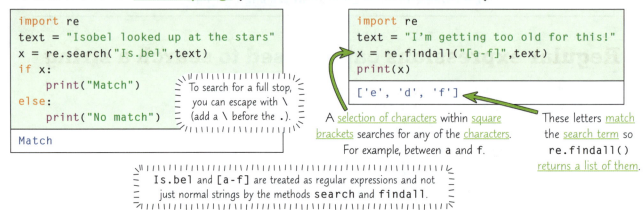

{2} indicates there should be exactly two capital letters in a row. {1,4} shows that there should be between one and four digits.

These first four user inputs failed as the regex didn't match because there were too few or too many characters, or they were the wrong type (e.g. yz not YZ).

3) Other examples of special characters include:

*	0 or more of the previous character	E.g. "xy*" would match for "x", "xy", and "xyyy".
?	0 or 1 of the previous character	E.g. "52?4" would match for "524", "54", but not "5224".
+	1 or more of the previous character	E.g. "abc+1" would match for "abc1","abccc1", but not "ab1".

I'll get a regular expression to go please... with milk...

Using regular expressions is pretty advanced — but even if you're able to use the basics it can save time when writing validation code. As ever, make sure to check any code you write to catch those pesky errors.

Section Nine — Making Programs Robust

Practice Questions and Activities

Q1 Give three ways you can validate a user input.

1 ....

2 ....

3 ....

Q2 A puzzle game asks for a 6-letter word to be typed in. Create a short program that does the following:

- Asks for a 6-letter word
- Checks the length to see if it is 6 characters
- Keeps asking for another word if the word entered isn't 6 characters
- Outputs 'thank you' when complete

Q3 The program shown sometimes produces an error. Describe why this happens and how it could be avoided.

```
month = int(input("What month is it?"))
print("Thank you")
```

....

....

....

Q4 Describe what regular expressions are used for.

....

....

Q5 Why are wildcards sometimes used within a search term?

....

....

Q6 The program on the right validates user input.

a) What is the likely purpose of this program?

```
import re
value = input("Input: ")
regex = "^£[0-9]+\.[0-9]{2}$"
check = re.search(regex,value)
while not check:
  value = input("Invalid. Input: ")
  check = re.search(regex,value)
print("Valid input.")
```

....

b) The following code is from line 3: `^£[0-9]+\.[0-9]{2}$`. Describe what the underlined parts mean.

....

....

....

c) Complete the test plan below with a range of sensible test data.

	Normal	Boundary	Erroneous
Examples			
Is it correctly validated by the program?			

Section Nine — Making Programs Robust

Debugging

Learning Objectives

Bugs can appear in your program at almost any point — that's why knowing how to debug code is extremely important. Here's a page on how to do it.

- Understand the meaning of the term 'debugging'.
- Understand common debugging and testing approaches.
- Understand the purpose of the pdb module.
- Use the pdb module to run a program one line at a time.

Debugging will help you to write error-free programs

1) Debugging code is the process of identifying and removing bugs.
2) A computer bug is an error in the code that causes it to fail in some way.
3) To produce robust programs you need to find and remove bugs.

Q1 Circle the four errors in the program below.

```
x = 3
y = 1
prinnt("There are",X+y,
errors in this program"(
```
Syntax error

Debugging should be taken seriously

1) Debugging usually happens as you write code, but once this is finished it's very important to test a program thoroughly. As you saw back in Section One, testing is a key part of the program design cycle (see p.11).
2) Testing can be done terminally (at the end of the development process) or iteratively (testing constantly during development).
3) Both types of testing might involve breaking your program into smaller chunks to be tested individually — this is called unit testing. Once you've finished unit testing, you should combine the individual units to check they work together — this is called integration testing.
4) You'll need to test your program under a range of conditions, including different test data (normal, boundary, invalid and erroneous) — see p.89.

The most difficult problems to debug don't create obvious errors — they might simply process the wrong data or not work well with an obscure boundary case.

Debuggers support the testing process

1) Most IDEs provide debugging tools, even if it's only syntax highlighting (when keywords are highlighted with different colours). Other tools include breakpoints (which stop execution at a certain point) and watches (which show you values changing as the program progresses).

2) These tools vary between different IDEs, but the Python Debugger module (pdb) has useful tools no matter which IDE you're using.

3) One of these is .set_trace(), which allows you to work through the code line by line.

When you run this program, there'll be some extra lines in the output that give the location of your Python file.

```
01  import pdb
02  pdb.set_trace()
03  print("Just adding things up")
04  a = 300
05  b = "Nineteen"
06  print("The total is:",a+b)
```

The breakpoint() function can also be used for debugging.

```
(Pdb) n
Just adding things up
(Pdb) n
-> a = 300
(Pdb) n
-> b = "Nineteen"
(Pdb) n
-> print("The answer is:",a+b)
(Pdb) n
TypeError: unsupported operand type(s) for +: 'int' and 'str'
```

Typing n (or next) executes the next line, outputting any print commands and displaying any variables.

This can be useful to pinpoint the exact moment a runtime or logic error occurs. This error shows that there's a problem with line 6.

Section Nine — Making Programs Robust

Exception Handling

Learning Objectives

Having a plan B is never a bad thing — it's always a good idea to be as well prepared as possible for unexpected events. Exception handling helps you deal with unexpected events

- Understanding the meaning of the term 'exception handling'.
- Understand how to use the `try` and `except` statements.
- Be able to add exception handling to a range of programs.

Exceptions prevent programs from executing normally

1) An error in a program triggers an exception — an abnormal event. Python lets you write backup code to run in case an exception happens — this would catch the issue before it could crash your program.

EXAMPLE The two key statements used to handle exceptions are `try` and `except`. Here's how they work.

Code nested inside `try` can be safely run. If an error occurs when running this code, an exception is triggered (raised) and the program flow jumps to the `except` block. Any other code in `try` will be ignored.

```
try:
    """ The code you
    want to try
    goes here. """

except:
    """ The backup code
    goes here. """
```

Code nested inside `except` responds to (catches) the exception. It will only run if an exception occurred in `try`. Once it's done, the program continues running any code after the `try`/`except` block.

2) Robust programs are written so that these exceptions can be caught and dealt with.
3) Syntax errors and logic errors should be debugged by you, but runtime errors can be anticipated and handled using exception handling `try` and `except` blocks.

Validation also helps prevent exceptions being triggered.

EXAMPLE A common runtime error is trying (and failing) to convert user input to be a float.

Validating floats is harder than integers since there isn't a direct equivalent of `.isdigit()`

```
num = float(input("Input: "))
```
```
Input: 5 point 5
ValueError: could not convert
string to float: '5 point 5'
```

This code validates the input to be a float by looping when an exception is raised.

```
while True:
    try:
        num = float(input("Input: "))
        break
    except:
        print("That was invalid.")
print("Success.")
```

If this line is reached it means there hasn't been an error, so the validation loop can end.

When a try...except block finishes, the program continues. It won't resume try after finishing except.

```
Input: 5 point 5
That was invalid.
Input: five point five?
That was invalid.
Input: 5.5
Success.
```

If this function can't convert to a float, an exception will be raised causing it to jump to `except` rather than executing `break`.

These first two inputs cause an exception to be raised but, crucially, the program doesn't crash.

4) Exception handling is helpful for dealing with all those annoying error messages but you should use it with caution.
5) In this code there would be a fatal NameError since codeNum doesn't exist, but because of the `try` and `except` the error doesn't appear. This means that exception handling isn't really helping — it's suppressing an error that should be fixed.

```
try:
    userName = "ABC"
    code = "2021"
    print(userName+codeNum)
except:
    print("Oopsie")
```
```
Oopsie
```

Section Nine — Making Programs Robust

Exception Handling

You can respond to specific errors in except blocks

EXAMPLE It's better practice to use try...except for small chunks when you're anticipating specific errors.

```
try:
    cricketScore = int(input("How many sixes did you hit? "))
    print("Excellent, that's",cricketScore * 6,"runs")
except ValueError:
    print("You must enter an integer.")
```

```
How many sixes did you hit? Three
You must enter an integer.
```

If the exception doesn't occur the program will still run as planned — except just won't be used.

As the string "Three" can't be cast as an integer, a ValueError is generated and the exception message is displayed.

You can add specific exception names to except.

```
# Assuming scores came from a user
scores = [5,4,"three",5,2]
try:
    average = sum(scores)/5
    print(average)
except TypeError:
    print("String value in list")
```

```
String value in list
```

The string in the list of integers causes the TypeError. This could be avoided in the first place by validating the input.

Assuming they're numbers, sum() adds up all of the items in the list.

Q1 Write a short program that responds to a ZeroDivisionError if the second of two divided integer inputs is zero.

More than one exception type can be used in a program

EXAMPLE Here's some game code that sets the character type and starting score of a player.

```
import random
def charLevel():
    while True:
        try:
            level = int(input("Choose an experience level from 0-10: "))
            if level > 10 or level < 0:
                print("Level should be between 0 and 10.")
            else:
                level = 1000 // level
                break
        except ZeroDivisionError:
            level = 1000
            break
        except ValueError:
            print("Make sure the level is a whole number.")
    return level

def charChoice():
    characters = ["Witch", "Dwarf", "Goblin"]
    choice = random.choice(characters)
    return choice

name = input("Please choose a name for your character: ")
level = charLevel()
choice = charChoice()
print("Your character,",name,", is a",choice,"and you'll start with",level,"game points.")
```

```
Please choose a name for your character: Glitbard
Choose an experience level from 0-10: 4
Your character, Glitbard , is a Goblin and
you'll start with 250 game points.
```

The user is asked to enter the experience level again if their first input was below zero or above 10.

Multiple except blocks are used to respond to potential errors — ZeroDivisionError and ValueError.

ZeroDivisionError occurs when an attempt is made to divide a number by zero.

ValueError occurs if the int function can't cast the user input to an integer.

The random.choice function is used to choose an item from the character list.

Q2 Why is the // operator used rather than / when calculating the number of game points?

Section Nine — Making Programs Robust

Practice Questions and Activities

Q1 Describe the meaning of the term debugging.

....

Q2 There are four errors in this short program. Circle the errors in the code and describe them.

Line 1 error: ....

Line 2 error: ....

Line 3 error: ....

Line 4 error: ....

```
01  %random number generator
02  inport random
03  num = random.ranint(0,100)
04  print(numb)
```

Q3 Describe what happens when the following code snippet is added to the start of a program.

```
import pdb
pdb.set_trace()
```

....

Q4 Explain the flow of execution in the program below when the user initially types in:

```
01  print("Please enter your GCSE grade:")
02
03  while True:
04      try:
05          grade = int(input())
06          while not (1 <= grade <= 9):
07              grade = int(input("Reenter: "))
08          break
09      except KeyboardInterrupt:
10          print("Enter a grade to end")
12      except ValueError:
13          print("You must enter an integer")
14
15  print("Your grade was",grade)
```

a) 7 ....

....

....

....

....

b) four ....

....

....

....

....

Q5 Explain why it's often better to use multiple `except` blocks that are specific to particular exceptions instead of using one generic `except` block.

....

....

....

....

....

Section Nine — Making Programs Robust

Coding Challenges for Section Nine

It's time to put your robustness to the test with some coding challenges. Once you're done with these challenges, head to the link on the contents page and download the Python programs that have been specially prepared.

Challenge 1

A pizza restaurant has developed an app for customers to order their pizzas online. When the order is placed, the app needs to check that the customer's mobile phone number has the correct format. You've been asked to write a program that does this.

Your program should:
- Ask the user to type in their mobile phone number.
- Confirm that the number starts with 0 or +44 and is followed by ten digits.
- Remove any spaces from the number.
- Before the program ends, print the number in an international format by replacing the first 0 with +44 if necessary.

Challenge 2

As part of a larger mathematics program, you've been asked to create a small program that carries out simple calculations with integers and includes exception handling.

Your program should:
- Include separate subroutines for addition and division calculations.
- Ask the user whether they want to do an ADD or DIVIDE.
- Include `ValueError` and `ZeroDivision` exception handling.
- Ask the user to re-enter the numbers in the calculation if what they entered is invalid.
- Keep asking to do more calculations and only end the program when the user types 'QUIT'.

Challenge 3

A manager at King's Cross Station wants a program which travellers can use to check the arrivals and departures at the station.

The program should:
- Ask the user whether they want to see arriving or departing trains.
- Show the details of 5 trains at a time, including the arriving or departing time of each train and which platform they are arriving at / leaving from.
- Ask the user if they want to see the details of 5 more trains once their original search is done.
- Repeat until the user says no to the above or there are no more trains to show.
- Include sufficient validation and exception handling throughout.

The details of each train can be loaded from a text file called 'trainsScheduled.txt'.

Challenge 4

You are part of a team creating an app for hiking expeditions. One feature of the app allows the hikers to record their position at various checkpoints, so that others are aware of their location.

The program should:
- Begin by asking the user for a current file name or if they want to create a new file.
- If they want to create a new file they should be asked to provide a file name.
- Keep asking the hiker for their coordinates until "Finished" is typed in.
- Coordinates entered must be in this format: (latitude,longitude).
  - The latitude degree expresses the North-South position and ranges from -90 to +90 inclusive.
  - The longitude degree expresses the East-West position and ranges from -180 to +180 inclusive.
  - Each degree can be expressed with up to 6 decimal places.
- If the current longitude or latitude is over 0.25 degrees higher or lower than the previous one entered, ask the user to confirm that this is correct before it's saved.
- Save each new coordinate in a file with the current date and time.

Here's a pair of sample co-ordinates:
Latitude: 27.9881
Longitude: 86.925

Section Ten — Algorithms and More Coding Challenges

Searching Algorithms

Learning Objectives: Some tasks are considered so fundamental to Computer Science that there are 'standard' algorithms for them. These include algorithms for searching and sorting.

- Understand the purpose of a searching algorithm.
- Understand the operation of linear and binary search algorithms and be able to implement them.
- Be able to compare the efficiency of linear and binary searches.

Searching is used to locate an item in a dataset

1) The purpose of a searching algorithm is to find a particular item within a group of multiple items. The terminology can vary a bit in this topic — the individual items can also be called elements, the group of items can also be called the dataset or just a list, and the item you're looking for can also be called the target.

2) Searching algorithms can be used to simply confirm whether this target item is within the dataset, or to find where exactly the target item is.

3) You've used searching earlier in the book, using built-in operations that use similar algorithms in order to work, such as:

```
myList.index("Target")      "Item" in myTuple      set1 & set2
```

Lists are referred to when talking about algorithms in this section, but other data structures can be used in these algorithms too.

4) Although there are ready-made searching tools, it's still important to understand what's going on behind the scenes. This is because you might find situations where they don't work how you need them to. So, for the time being at least, we're going to pretend they don't exist...

Searching isn't a straightforward task for a computer

1) This topic hasn't slipped into the final section by mistake — although searching is often an easy task for us, for a computer it requires more careful consideration. For example, searching for Penguin in this dataset:

Target: Penguin   Dataset: Turtle, Elephant, Cheetah, Penguin, Wolf

2) You can almost instantly spot Penguin in the second to last position — but that's because you are able to quickly take in the list, or perhaps your eye was just drawn to the target word straight away.

3) A computer can only consider one item at a time and so, even for a small dataset like the one above, it would need to use a far more careful, systematic approach to find the target.

Linear search takes things step-by-step

1) The linear search algorithm follows the simplest approach to searching — checking every single item, one by one, until you find the target item.

2) That's how you might have, even without realising, found Penguin in the list above. If you have to use an unordered list, then linear search is the only option. Even for us as humans, if the dataset is much bigger there's not much else we can do either.

Python generally uses linear search in most of its searching operations (with some optimisations for efficiency).

> **Q1** Define a function called linearSearch to perform this algorithm. It should have two parameters: one is the list to be searched and the other is the target item. If the item exists in the list, then return its index. If it doesn't exist, return -1. Test this function using the animal dataset above.
>
> **Q2** Extend your code for Q1 so that this function works with both 1D and 2D lists as arguments.

Searching Algorithms

Binary search is more complex than linear search

1) It involves comparing the middle item (also called the pivot) to the target, using this to discard half of the list, and repeating the process until you've found the target or it runs out of items to check.

   Binary search is similar to how you might use a (real) dictionary.

2) This might not make much sense until you take a look at an example — see below.

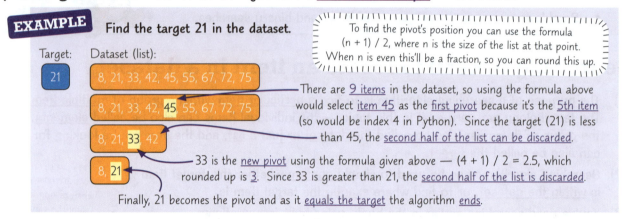

EXAMPLE Find the target 21 in the dataset.

Target: 21

Dataset (list): 8, 21, 33, 42, 45, 55, 67, 72, 75

To find the pivot's position you can use the formula (n + 1) / 2, where n is the size of the list at that point. When n is even this'll be a fraction, so you can round this up.

There are 9 items in the dataset, so using the formula above would select item 45 as the first pivot because it's the 5th item (so would be index 4 in Python). Since the target (21) is less than 45, the second half of the list can be discarded.

33 is the new pivot using the formula given above — (4 + 1) / 2 = 2.5, which rounded up is 3. Since 33 is greater than 21, the second half of the list is discarded.

Finally, 21 becomes the pivot and as it equals the target the algorithm ends.

3) Linear search works just fine on lists that have no order, but for binary search the items must be arranged in order, as the algorithm relies on being able to reject half of the list with certainty that the target isn't there.

4) The list in the example above was numerical and in ascending order. It could have equally been in descending order or have been in alphabetical order if it was a list of strings — you'd just need to adapt to those other cases when implementing the algorithm.

> **Q3** Define a function called `binarySearch` to perform this algorithm. It should have two parameters — one is the list to be searched and one is the target item. If the item exists in the list, then return its index. If it doesn't exist, return -1. Test this function using the numerical dataset above. You can assume that the list is in ascending order.

Some algorithms are more efficient than others

1) Measures of algorithmic efficiency are separate from how quickly it runs in practice. Timing an algorithm may give you an idea of its efficiency, but timings can change under different conditions — e.g. depending on the performance of the computer.

2) Instead, efficiency is often analysed by looking at how many steps are taken and how much memory space the algorithm will take up in the average-case and the worst-case scenarios. The best-case often isn't interesting — since that would be if the search algorithm found the item straight away.

3) This graph shows roughly how these two algorithms compare as the size of a list grows. When the list is small the performance is very similar. However, when the list gets bigger binary search requires far fewer steps than linear search.

4) This is because when the size of a list doubles, binary search only needs to 'compare and discard' one extra time whereas the linear search has twice as many items to potentially go through. So when a list is large, using binary search makes a big difference.

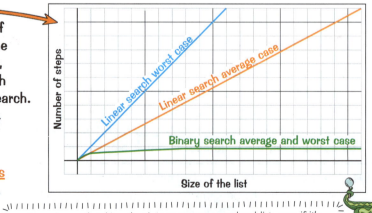

It can be worth taking the time to sort an unordered list, even if it's large, so it'll work with binary search rather than the slower linear search.

Sorting Algorithms

Learning Objectives

Linear and binary search are the main algorithms used for searching. But for sorting it's a bit more crowded — we're going to look at three of the most common sorting algorithms.

- Understand the purpose of a sorting algorithm.
- Understand the operation of the bubble, merge and insertion sorting algorithms and be able to implement them.
- Be able to compare the efficiency of different sorting algorithms.

Sorting puts a list in order

1) Sorting helps organise data and makes it easier to use. It can also be used to speed up searching.
2) The examples and tasks here are just going to be sorting lists in ascending or descending order, either with numerical or text data. This is what most (but not all) real life sorting tasks will be too.

Bubble sort looks at each pair and swaps them if needed

1) The bubble sort algorithm follows a simple principle — go through the list looking at each pair and if the items in that pair are out of order, swap them.
2) Each time the algorithm works its way through a list doing these swaps it's called a pass. The algorithm keeps doing these passes until a pass is completed with no swaps which means the list must be sorted.

EXAMPLE Sort the list below into ascending order using a bubble sort.

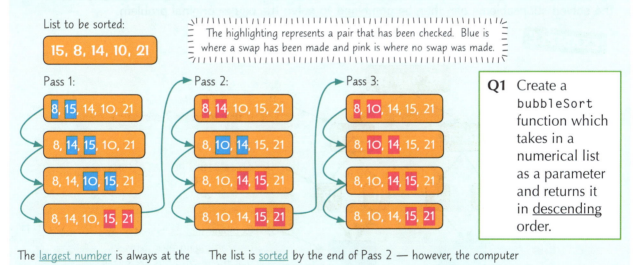

Q1 Create a `bubbleSort` function which takes in a numerical list as a parameter and returns it in descending order.

Q2 The algorithm is called bubble sort because items 'bubble' towards the end as they get sorted. Modify the function you created in Q1 to ensure that efficiency is maximised by reducing the number of comparisons after each pass.

Who knew bubbles had anything to do with programming...?

So you've learnt about bubbles being used for sorting, but we're not done yet. There's another two algorithms on the next couple of pages to get your teeth (or maybe fins?) into. Go on, get sorting...

Section Ten — Algorithms and More Coding Challenges

Sorting Algorithms

Insertion sort sorts the list one item at a time

1) Insertion sort splits a list into a sorted and an unsorted part.
2) Items are added one-by-one to the sorted part — this makes sure that new items are inserted in the correct place.

Some implementations use separate sorted and unsorted lists — items are moved from the unsorted list into the sorted one.

EXAMPLE Here's the insertion sort algorithm as a flow chart.

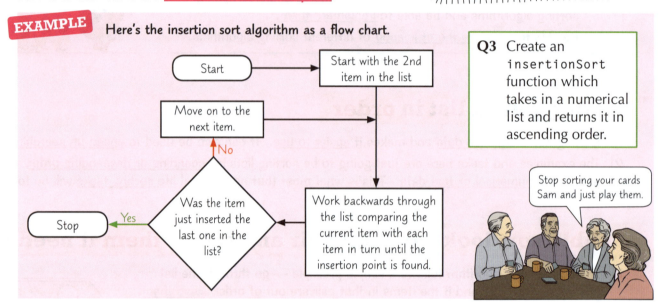

Q3 Create an `insertionSort` function which takes in a numerical list and returns it in ascending order.

Stop sorting your cards Sam and just play them.

Merge sort divides before it merges

Merge sort is an example of a divide and conquer algorithm — these types of algorithms work by breaking down a problem repeatedly until the subproblems become easy enough to solve. The solved subproblems can then be combined to solve the bigger original problem.

EXAMPLE Here's how merge sort works with a short list.

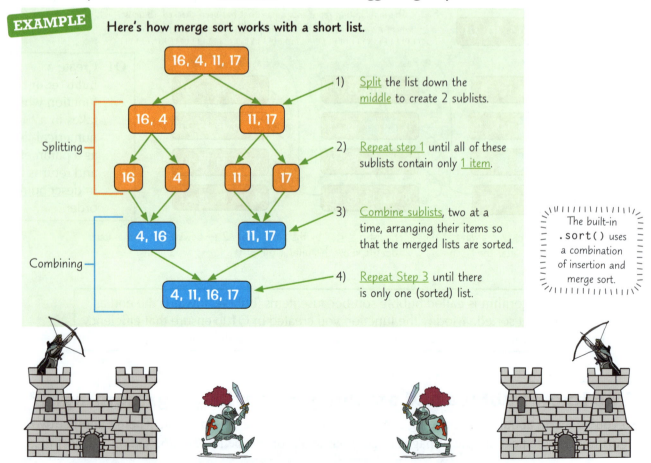

1) Split the list down the middle to create 2 sublists.
2) Repeat step 1 until all of these sublists contain only 1 item.
3) Combine sublists, two at a time, arranging their items so that the merged lists are sorted.
4) Repeat Step 3 until there is only one (sorted) list.

The built-in .sort() uses a combination of insertion and merge sort.

103

Sorting Algorithms

Merge sort is usually solved recursively

This is a tricky concept so here's some annotated pseudocode to guide you through it.

EXAMPLE This pseudocode is for numerical lists which are to be sorted in ascending order.

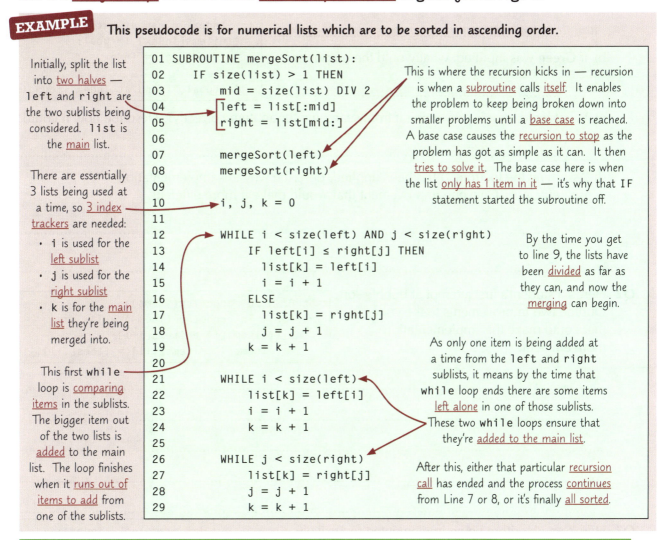

Initially, split the list into two halves — left and right are the two sublists being considered. list is the main list.

There are essentially 3 lists being used at a time, so 3 index trackers are needed:
- i is used for the left sublist
- j is used for the right sublist
- k is for the main list they're being merged into.

This first while loop is comparing items in the sublists. The bigger item out of the two lists is added to the main list. The loop finishes when it runs out of items to add from one of the sublists.

```
01  SUBROUTINE mergeSort(list):
02      IF size(list) > 1 THEN
03          mid = size(list) DIV 2
04          left = list[:mid]
05          right = list[mid:]
06
07          mergeSort(left)
08          mergeSort(right)
09
10          i, j, k = 0
11
12          WHILE i < size(left) AND j < size(right)
13              IF left[i] ≤ right[j] THEN
14                  list[k] = left[i]
15                  i = i + 1
16              ELSE
17                  list[k] = right[j]
18                  j = j + 1
19              k = k + 1
20
21          WHILE i < size(left)
22              list[k] = left[i]
23              i = i + 1
24              k = k + 1
25
26          WHILE j < size(right)
27              list[k] = right[j]
28              j = j + 1
29              k = k + 1
```

This is where the recursion kicks in — recursion is when a subroutine calls itself. It enables the problem to keep being broken down into smaller problems until a base case is reached. A base case causes the recursion to stop as the problem has got as simple as it can. It then tries to solve it. The base case here is when the list only has 1 item in it — it's why that IF statement started the subroutine off.

By the time you get to line 9, the lists have been divided as far as they can, and now the merging can begin.

As only one item is being added at a time from the left and right sublists, it means by the time that while loop ends there are some items left alone in one of those sublists. These two while loops ensure that they're added to the main list.

After this, either that particular recursion call has ended and the process continues from Line 7 or 8, or it's finally all sorted.

Q4 Create a mergeSort function which takes in a numerical list and sorts it in descending order.

Merge sort is time efficient

1) The graph on the right shows how the different sorting algorithms generally perform as a list grows — you'll see that merge sort quickly outperforms bubble and insertion sort. However, when the lists are small, the difference in performance is minor.

2) Merge sort isn't perfect though — the use of sublists means it uses more memory space than the other two, and its implementation is less straightforward to understand and code.

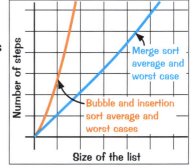

Q5 Generate a list of 10000 random integers, each between 1 and 10000. Use the time module to compare the running times of bubble, insertion and merge sort on this list, using the functions you created in Qs 2, 3 and 4. You'll need to modify them so they all sort ascending.

Sorting... You might find it sorta fun...

Pseudocode might not seem that useful outside of your exams but it's worth remembering that it can be useful for writing out tricky algorithms like merge sort. Go back to Section One for a refresher about it.

Section Ten — Algorithms and More Coding Challenges

Practice Questions and Activities

Q1 This code implements a searching algorithm but it's not working properly.

```
items = ("Red","Green","Purple","Yellow")
goal = input("Enter the search term: ")

for index in range(len(items)):
    if items[index] != goal:
        foundIndex = index

print(goal,"found at index",foundIndex)
```

a) Which searching algorithm does it most closely resemble?

....

b) If **Green** was inputted, what would the output be?

....

c) What logic error is preventing it from searching for an item correctly? Describe how it could be fixed.

....

d) Assuming the fix from c) has been applied, describe why this implementation isn't efficient. Give one improvement that would make it more efficient.

....

....

Q2 Here's a student's first attempt at bubble sort. Outline two improvements to the code that could make this implementation more efficient.

```
for Pass in range(len(items)):
    for i in range(len(items) - 1):
        if items[i] > items[i+1]:
            items[i], items[i+1] = items[i+1], items[i]
```

....

....

....

....

Q3 Here's an algorithm being implemented recursively.

```
def example(L, index):
    item = L[index]
    j = index
    while j > 0 and L[j-1] < item:
        L[j] = L[j-1]
        j -= 1
    L[j] = item
    if index + 1 <= len(L) - 1:
        example(L, index+1)
    return L
myList = example([4,1,91,7,14], 1)
print(myList)
```

a) Name the algorithm used in the code.

Warning: this question is a tricky one.

....

b) Give the output of this code.

....

c) Describe how recursion has been used.

....

....

....

Q4 A local council have parsed a CSV file to create a list of all house sale prices over the last 40 years. They need to search for the cheapest and most expensive house sales in this time. Evaluate the different options they have.

Answer this one on a separate piece of paper.

Advanced Coding Challenges

The challenges on the next few pages bring together everything you've learned in this book — they're a significant step up in length and complexity. So don't expect to be solving them in 5 minutes — think of each one as a mini-project to really get your teeth into. Time to flex those fingers...

Top Tips

Don't forget to head to the link on the contents page to get those Python programs and text files.

Before you get started, here are some top tips:

1) Read carefully through the whole of the task before getting going — make sure you understand what's being asked before you dive in.

2) Do some planning beforehand — this might be:
   - Drawing a quick flowchart on paper
   - Writing some pseudocode for any tricky-sounding parts
   - Jotting down what variables and data structures you might need
   - Deciding what subroutines you'll define yourself

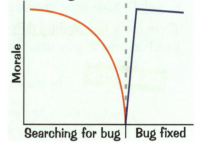

3) When you're ready to get coding, don't try and solve each task all in one go. Focus on breaking it down into smaller parts that are more manageable.

4) Aim to implement the good programming practice tips scattered throughout this book — such as using descriptive variable names, writing comments for yourself, programming defensively and using subroutines wherever possible. This'll make your life much easier.

5) If you get stuck on a particular section of code, don't be afraid to look back through this book or do some searching for specific techniques online. Also, sometimes taking a break from a problem and coming back to it later is all you need for that eureka moment to happen.

Challenge 1 — Snowman guessing game

Snowman is an alternative version of the game 'hangman'. In the game a word is selected and those playing the game guess letters that could be in the word. When a player guesses a correct letter the position(s) of this letter in the word are revealed. When a player guesses wrongly, a 'try' is used.

Your game should work as follows:

1) The program chooses a random word from the 'dictionary.txt' provided. In Easy mode, this should be 5 letters or less. In Medium mode, this should be between 6 and 10 letters (inclusive). In Difficult mode, the word selected is 11 or more letters.

2) Once the word is selected — the user is shown the number of letters in underscore form. E.g. if 'snowball' was selected, the user would see _ _ _ _ _ _ _ _

3) The user keeps guessing letters or, if they're feeling brave, the whole word. If they guess a single letter and they were correct, reveal where that letter is within the word. E.g. if the user guessed 'l' then the display would be _ _ _ _ _ _ l l.

4) If they guess more than one letter, treat this as a guess of the word itself. Either they are totally correct or totally wrong.

5) The case of the guesses doesn't matter (so 'l' is the same as 'L').

6) Each time a user guesses a letter wrong, display the previously incorrect letters alongside the hidden word. Don't let them guess this letter again. For either a wrong letter or a wrong word guess, show that a try has been used by displaying the following stages of a snowman being built using ASCII art:

   1) bottom snowball
   2) middle snowball
   3) head snowball
   4) face
   5) branches and buttons
   6) top hat

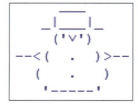

This is just an example snowman — yours doesn't need to match it exactly. Just make sure the list of stages on the left are needed to build it.

7) After the top hat has been added, it's game over for the user. They win if they guess correctly before all stages of the snowman build are complete.

Advanced Coding Challenges

Challenge 2 — Denary-binary converter

Denary is also called decimal.

Denary and binary are two interchangeable number systems. Binary is used to represent denary numbers in computers. Binary uses only 2 digits (0 and 1), so is also called base-2, whereas denary is base-10.

You should create a program that lets a user provide a denary integer and receive the binary equivalent. The program should also provide the option to do the reverse process — converting a binary integer to its denary equivalent. As an extension, you could also allow conversion between other bases, like hexadecimal or octal. Your code should perform these without the use of any built-in conversion functions.

There are a few slightly different ways to perform conversions between number systems — it doesn't matter which approach you use. Here's how the place value in these number systems works:

EXAMPLE The place value of denary multiplies by 10 as it moves right to left, starting from 1.

This table shows the place values of the digits in the denary number 10527.

10000	1000	100	10	1
1	0	5	2	7

The place value of binary doubles as it moves right to left, starting from 1.

This table shows the place value of the digits in the binary number 10110110. The top row shows the denary value each digit represents.

128	64	32	16	8	4	2	1
1	0	1	1	0	1	1	0

You can use the place values to convert between the bases. → 128 + 32 + 16 + 4 + 2 = 182. → So, the binary 10110110 is 182 in denary.

Challenge 3 — Mersenne primes

A prime number is an integer greater than 1 that doesn't have any factors apart from 1 and itself. A Mersenne prime is a special kind of prime number that is 1 less than a power of 2.

EXAMPLE
13 is a prime number, since only 1 and 13 divide into it without a remainder.

14 isn't a prime number since 1, 2, 7 and 14 are factors.

127 is an example of a Mersenne prime since 127 is a prime number and also $2^7 - 1 = 127$.

At the time of writing, only 51 Mersenne primes are known. Your program should find the 10 smallest of these. Depending on your computer's performance and the efficiency of your algorithm, you may be able to generate more.

You may not need this, but the following may help you develop an efficient solution:
- The exponent (P) of the $2^P - 1$, must be prime for the number to be a Mersenne prime.
- One algorithm that tests if a value of P can lead to a Mersenne prime is the Lucas-Lehmer test. This states that, when P is bigger than 2, $2^P - 1$ must be a Mersenne prime if S_{P-2} is 0 when this sequence is calculated: $S_0 = 4$, $S_n = (S_{n-1}^2 - 2) \bmod (2^P - 1)$.
Complicated stuff, I know. Here's an example of using this test on 127 (which is $2^7 - 1$, so P = 7):

EXAMPLE Using the Lucas-Lehmer test to prove that 127 is a Mersenne prime.

$S_0 = 4$ # Always start with 4 as the first term.
$S_1 = (4^2 - 2) \bmod 127 = 14$ # Use the previous result when calculating future terms.
$S_2 = (14^2 - 2) \bmod 127 = 67$
$S_3 = (67^2 - 2) \bmod 127 = 42$ # Keep going until you reach S_{P-2} (here, P = 7 so that is S_5).
$S_4 = (42^2 - 2) \bmod 127 = 111$
$S_5 = (111^2 - 2) \bmod 127 = 0$ # Since S_{P-2} is 0, 127 is a Mersenne prime. Otherwise, it's not.

Advanced Coding Challenges

Challenge 4 — Run-length encoding

<u>Lossless compression</u> is used to <u>reduce</u> the size of files <u>without deleting</u> any of the original content. The idea is to apply an algorithm that can <u>store the data more efficiently</u>, but in a way that allows the file to be restored to its <u>original form after it's decompressed</u>.

EXAMPLE Run-length encoding (RLE) is an example of a lossless compression algorithm. Here's how it works.

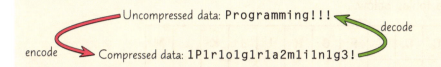

<u>Encoding</u> involves <u>counting</u> how many times each character <u>immediately repeats itself</u> as you go through the data — any repeats are called '<u>runs</u>', e.g. there's a run of 3 '!'s in the uncompressed data.

Assuming 8 bit ASCII, the <u>uncompressed data</u> would take up <u>112 bits</u> — for each of the 14 characters, they'll be stored using <u>8 binary digits</u> (bits). In comparison, the <u>compressed RLE data</u> will take up <u>176 bits</u>. So, because this example didn't have many (or long) runs of the same character, applying the algorithm would have the <u>opposite effect</u> to what was intended.

Your program should be able to implement **RLE** with the following features:

1) An option for the user to either <u>encode or decode</u> their input as **RLE**.
2) An option to <u>estimate how much space was saved</u> (or not) through applying **RLE**, based on the example above.
3) An option for the user to <u>specify a file path</u> and either <u>encode or decode</u> their file as **RLE**. A <u>new file</u> should be created in either case.
   - For the <u>encoding</u> option, only output the compressed data if applying RLE would be <u>beneficial</u>. If it doesn't reduce the file size, it should inform the user of this.
   - For the <u>decoding</u> option, this should also work if the RLE compression is in one of these alternative formats:

     (1,h),(2,i),(4,!)   ... should be decoded as: hii!!!!
     (h,1),(i,2),(!,4)   ... should also be decoded as: hii!!!!

You can assume the text won't include numbers — but the algorithm should work with symbols.

For this challenge you can use 'exampleUncompressed1.txt' and 'exampleUncompressed2.txt' as example .txt files. These can be found at the download link on the contents page.

Challenge 5 — Turtle graphics cityscape

Use methods from the <u>Turtle library</u> to create artwork of a city skyline or street scene.
Make sure your artwork contains the following features:

- At least <u>four buildings</u> — two of which should be of a <u>different design</u>.
- An option for the user to control the <u>number of floors</u> of at least one of these buildings.
- An option for the user to control the <u>colour</u> of at least one of these buildings.
- At least one <u>non-building item on display</u> — e.g. the Sun, the Moon, a bird, a car or a person.
- An aspect of <u>random generation</u>, so that every time the program runs it will be slightly different. This could be something like the position of an item, the colour of an item or the dimensions of the item.

You can use `speed()` *to change the speed of the turtle drawing.*

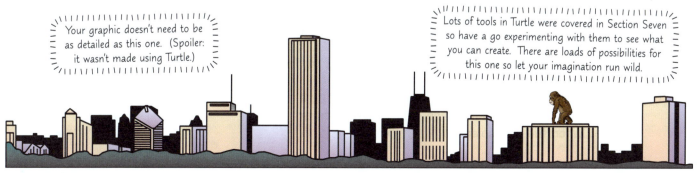

Your graphic doesn't need to be as detailed as this one. (Spoiler: it wasn't made using Turtle.)

Lots of tools in Turtle were covered in Section Seven so have a go experimenting with them to see what you can create. There are loads of possibilities for this one so let your imagination run wild.

Section Ten — Algorithms and More Coding Challenges

Advanced Coding Challenges

Challenge 6 — Vigenère cipher

Encryption is when data is made unreadable to unauthorised viewers. Authorised viewers are given a key (usually a string of numbers or letters) which they can use to decrypt the data — i.e. make the data readable.

Data can be encrypted using the Vigenère cipher — one example of an encryption algorithm (cipher). Here's how this cipher works:

1) Each letter in the alphabet is given a value according to its position. Use the values given in the tables below.

A	B	C	D	E	F	G	H	I	J	K	L	M
0	1	2	3	4	5	6	7	8	9	10	11	12

N	O	P	Q	R	S	T	U	V	W	X	Y	Z
13	14	15	16	17	18	19	20	21	22	23	24	25

Z doesn't have a value of 26 which you might expect, because A has a value of 0.

2) Each letter in the original word, called the plaintext, is shifted along the alphabet by the same number of places as the value of the letter held in the key. This results in a mix of characters called the ciphertext, which is unreadable, unless you know the key and can do the reverse process to decrypt it.

EXAMPLE Encrypting the plaintext 'PYTHON' with the key 'THEKEY' gives the ciphertext 'IFXRSL'.

PLAINTEXT	P	Y	T	H	O	N
	15	24	19	7	14	13
KEY	T	H	E	K	E	Y
	19	7	4	10	4	24
CIPHERTEXT	I	F	X	R	S	L
	8	5	23	17	18	11

To create the ciphertext character for P you add the value of T (19) to the value of P (15) — 15 + 19 = 34. This number is more than 25 (beyond the value that represents Z) so to get to position 34 you need to go past Z and back to the start of the alphabet — you can do this by counting 19 steps on from P or by subtracting 26 from 34. You should get a value of 8, which represents I.

If your ciphertext value is less than 25 it's just a case of matching the number to the letter — 7 + 10 = 17 which represents R.

Your program should meet the following requirements:
1) There should be an option for a user to encrypt a message using the Vigenère cipher. They should be able to either provide a key or have a random one generated for them.
2) For simplicity, the key should always be the same length as the plaintext and the plaintext should be without spaces or punctuation.
3) There should be an option for a user to decrypt a message using a key they provide. Ensure the key is the same length as the ciphertext.
4) Always provide the ciphertext in capital letters.
5) There should be a menu to choose between encrypting a message and decrypting a message. The program should only end when the user selects a 'Quit' option.

As an extension task, try allowing the key to be less than the length of the plain/cipher texts. In this case, it should repeat.

Advanced Coding Challenges

Challenge 7 — Breaking Vigenère

The implementation of Vigenère in Challenge 6 is very similar to a Vernam cipher. A Vernam cipher (also called a One-Time Pad) offers perfect security — it cannot be broken if the key is random and is as at least as long as the plaintext. However, if a key has been used more than once, there's an opportunity to crack the encryption.

Vigenère has been used to encrypt two 9-letter words from a text file (vigenereWords.txt) which contains thousands of 9-letter words. The same random 9-letter key has been used to encrypt both words and the resulting ciphertext is shown here.

Your challenge is to devise an attack against the encryption so you can figure out the original plaintexts and the key that was used. You should reuse code from Challenge 6 to help write your program.

Ciphertext 1: CDAUXMCFE
Ciphertext 2: VFQJTCQCN

Challenge 8 — Lottery draw

Create a program which can be used to manage a simple lottery. To take part in a lottery, players buy a lottery ticket which has numbers on. When the lottery draw is made, a sequence of numbers is randomly chosen. If these numbers match the numbers on a player's ticket then they've won. A ticket in this lottery has 5 numbers from 0 to 9. The same number can appear more than once.

Your program should do the following:

1) Allow the user to navigate to the features below via a menu. The program should only end when the 'Quit' option is selected.

2) Allow the user to register that a player has bought a ticket. Depending on what the player chooses, either give them a random selection of 5 numbers or let them enter their specified numbers. Either way, ensure that the numbers don't match with a ticket that's already been bought. The name of the player and their lottery numbers must be stored in an external text file.

3) Allow the user to run the lottery draw in order to select a winner. The user should be able to select one of two winning options:
    1) The winner must have the exact numbers in the same order as those that are randomly generated by the program. There may be no winner.
    2) One player is picked at random, regardless of their numbers.

4) Have an option that will display the odds of a single ticket winning the lottery. Express this as a percentage for both of the winning options outlined above.

You can download an example text file from the link on the contents page.

Challenge 9 — Frequency analysis

Create a program which can be used to conduct frequency analysis on text. It should work with any .txt file, but you can use the provided romeoAndJuliet.txt as an example.

Your program should do the following:
- Read a text file.
- Output to the user the most used word and also how many words are used in total.
- Assume a word is anything non-numerical which is next to a single space.
- Punctuation should be ignored, as should the capitalisation of a word.
- After the above information is outputted, allow the user to enter any word and show them how many times it occurs in the text.
- Keep repeating this option until they type in -1.

Once you have completed this you could attempt the following extension tasks:
- Conduct frequency analysis on individual letters as well as words.
- Show the most frequent n words, as specified by the user — e.g. the top 5 most frequent words.
- Plot the top n words and/or letters on a graph. This could be done using the module matplotlib — this module isn't included by default in most Python distributions so you might need to install it separately.

Section Ten — Algorithms and More Coding Challenges

Ideas for Advanced Coding Projects

Amazing job if you've got this far — however, hopefully your programming journey isn't over yet. Here are some ideas for other projects you could try which will need to use concepts that go beyond those covered in this book. For each idea, there are some suggestions for which concepts you could have a look into.

Flash cards with a GUI

With the exception of turtle graphics, all the programs in this book have resulted in a command-line interface (CLI). However, most programs which are distributed to users have a graphical user interface (GUI). The default GUI module for Python is Tkinter (which IDLE is written in) but wxPython and PyQt are alternatives.

You could create a program which allows you to revise a subject, like Computer Science, using flash cards on a screen. Key terms and their definitions could be loaded in from an external file randomly to be shown to the user in a GUI window. The user could be shown a term, take a moment to think of the definition and then 'flip' the card to check whether their definition was correct.

Social media analysis using machine learning

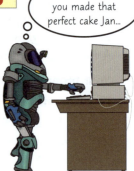

No one believes you made that perfect cake Jan...

Machine learning (ML) is an area of artificial intelligence in which algorithms take in lots of data and try to make predictions based on it. Python is used a lot for ML — good free modules include scikit-learn and TensorFlow. These may need to be installed on your computer to use — a distribution like Anaconda® can help with this.

A common ML project is performing sentiment analysis, which is where the ML tries to learn the emotions in some text. Social media can provide lots of data for you to use — as a starting point, you could see what datasets are freely available to download, or obtain the data yourself using an API (application programming interface) provided by a social media company like Twitter or YouTube™.

Database-driven management information systems

Those may be the 5 most boring words it's possible to put together, but they're important for storing lots of data. Large scale programs don't store data in text files as you've seen earlier in the book, they use databases instead. An example of a management information system (MIS) would be something like the system your school may use to take registers and store details about staff and students. This will require multiple database tables linked together with key fields. A database module like sqlite3 can be used to manage this in Python.

Using OOP to recreate card games

Object-oriented programming (OOP) is a popular approach to programming which Python supports but doesn't require you to follow. Terminology you've come across earlier in the book like referring to variables and data structures as 'objects' and the use of the 'method' subroutines actually belong to OOP. But there are some other key OOP concepts not covered in this book.

Many of the longer coding exercises could be re-written in an OOP way, but if you fancy a brand new project, you could try to replicate a card game like Blackjack or Rummy.

Sending encrypted messages across networks

Socket programming is setting up a connection between your computer and another computer. This can be used to set up a client-server or a peer-to-peer network. You could use the socket module to set up a test connection with yourself or another computer if you have access to one. To practise exchanging the data, you could use an encryption algorithm like Vigenère or a more advanced one like AES, which is used for real-life symmetric encryption.

Section Ten — Algorithms and More Coding Challenges

Answers

Section One — Introduction to Python

Page 2 — What is Python?
Q1 E.g.
- web development
- education/teaching programming
- graphical user interfaces (GUIs)
- business applications

Page 4 — The Shell Window
Q1 20

Pages 9-10 — Representing Algorithms
Q1 E.g.
1) Put water in kettle
2) Boil kettle
3) Get a mug ready
4) Put a teaspoon of coffee in mug
5) Put boiling water in mug
6) Add milk if required
7) Stir coffee

Q2 E.g. Flowcharts are the visual representation of an algorithm and are used to plan a program and the flow of data.
Pseudocode is a simple code-like language that uses English terms to describe common programming functions and structure. It can be easily converted to a real programming language, like Python.

Page 11 — The Program Design Cycle
Q1 E.g.
- How easy the program is to use.
- Whether the program solves the original problem.
- If there any ways the program could be improved.

Section Two — Inputs, Outputs and Variables

Page 14 — Variables
Q1 You should've crossed out:
`3rdPlace = "Jack"`
`vegan? = "Yes"`
`favourite planet = "Neptune"`

Page 15 — Practice Questions and Activities
Q1 E.g.
`print"Hello World!)`
`print("Hello")World!`

Q2 A variable is a name that is used to represent a value. The value assigned to the variable is held by the computer, meaning that it can be used later on in the program. You can change the value of the variable by re-assigning it.

Q3 a) A variable could be used to keep track of the height of the sunflower — such as `flowerHeight`. You could also use a variable to keep track of time — such as `daysElapsed`.

b) You could use six variables to keep track of each player's score in each level, e.g. `playerOne_L1`, `playerTwo_L1` (and the same for levels 2 and 3). A total variable can be used for each player, such as `playerOne_totalPoints` — this would be used to keep track of all the points accumulated by each player.

Q4 a) 5
b) Error
Line three is invalid as the variable name needs to be on the left of the equals sign.
c) 9

Q5 `profit` is initialised as `0`
`revenue` is initialised as `10000`
`totalCosts` is initialised as `4000`
`profit` is assigned the result of `10000` minus `4000`, which is `6000`
The final value of `profit` is outputted to the user's screen.
Output: `The profit is 6000`

Page 17 — Getting User Inputs
Q1 E.g. you could add in the following lines of code.
```
age = input("How old are you? ")
print("Wow, you look good for",age)
favColour = input("What's your favourite colour? ")
print("Even at",age,"you like",favColour,"?")
dreamJob = input("Last question: what's your dream job? ")
print("Nice, I can see you doing",dreamJob,name)
```

You can download a complete example program from cgpbooks.co.uk/GCSEPythonExtras

Answers

Q2
```
The number is 12
Enter a number: Hello World
What is your message? 41
41 Hello World
```

Page 19 — Practice Questions and Activities

Q1 E.g. To be able to receive information that the user types in via their keyboard. The program can be made to run differently based on what the user enters.

Q2 E.g. Variables allow what the user types in to be held by the computer. Using variables also means you can represent future inputs when coding, despite not knowing what will be entered until runtime.

Q3 a)
```
What's your pet's name? Greg
What animal is Greg? Carp
You called your Carp Greg?!
```

b)
```
5
2nd input: 7
Enter a separator: 2
527212
```

Q4 `print("\"One\", \\Two\n\t\"Three\"")`

Q5 Errors in the program have been circled.
```
print("I am a sentient chatbot.")
1stName = Input("What's your name, BTW? ")
print("I'm sensing your name is.../n"+1stName)
```

Line 2 errors: variable name isn't valid as it starts with a number, input shouldn't start with a capital 'I', there's a missing quotation mark (") after the '('.
Line 3 errors: the forward slash should be a backslash, variable name is invalid.
The corrected code:
```
print("I am a sentient chatbot.")
firstName = input("What's your name, BTW? ")
print("I'm sensing your name is...\n"+firstName)
```

Q6 Advantage: e.g. this gives the user the whole line free to type in the input OR the prompt is on the line above which can aid readability.
Disadvantage: e.g. it takes up two lines instead of one.

Page 20 — Coding Challenges for Section Two

Head to cgpbooks.co.uk/GCSEPythonExtras to download an example program for each challenge.

Section Three — Data Types and Operations

Pages 21-22 — Data Types

Q1

Example	Data Type
-12.01	Float
"Leafy Lane"	String
True	Boolean

Q2 3827
14.44
1010

Page 23 — Arithmetic Operators

Q1 It would allow decimal points to be used.

Pages 24-25 — Practice Questions and Activities

Q1

Value	String	Boolean	Float
16.5			✓
Big Wednesday	✓		
false	✓		

'false' isn't Boolean because Boolean logic is case sensitive so it would need to be 'False' in order for it to be Boolean.

Q2 a) E.g. A positive or negative whole number without a decimal point.
b) E.g. A combination of letters, numbers and symbols in any order.
c) E.g. Any positive or negative number — including those with a decimal point.

Q3 a) 16
b) E.g. To assign a particular data type to a value.

Q4 a) integer
b) float
c) string
d) boolean

Q5 E.g. This program asks the user for a number and then carries out a series of calculations. No matter what number is entered, the calculations will always result in an output of `2.0`.

Q6 Errors in the program have been circled.
```
width = int(input("Enter the width in metres: "))
height = input("Enter the height in metres: "))
area = width x height
print("The area is",area "square metres.")
```

First error: Missing `int(` before `input(` in line 2.
Second error: Use of `x` instead of `*` for multiplication.
Third error: Missing comma after `area` variable.
The corrected program:
```
width = int(input("Enter the width in metres: "))
height = int(input("Enter height in metres: "))
area = width * height
print("The area is",area,"square metres.")
```

Answers

Q7 a) 100
 b) 65
 c) 9.0
 d) 25
 e) 4
 f) 1

Page 28 — Boolean Operators
Q1 `Are you a winner? False`

Page 29 — String Handling
Q1 Missing line: `letterS = word.count("s")`
Output: 4

Pages 31-32 — Practice Questions and Activities
Q1 Any two examples with valid descriptions, e.g.
- Central heating turning on or off when set to a specific temperature.
- Age restricted websites and applications allowing access if a user is over a certain age.
- Airport luggage scales letting you know if your suitcase is too heavy.
- Adaptive cruise control systems in cars accelerating or braking to maintain a constant speed.

Q2 a) less than or equal to
 b) not equal to
 c) exactly equal to

Q3 `Target speed exceeded: False`

Q4 a)
```
250 > 240
True
```
 b)
```
1000 == 1000
True
```
 c)
```
1999 != 1999
False
```

Q5 Any three from: e.g.
- changing the case
- counting characters
- string slicing
- concatenation

Q6 a) `Tea`
 b) `for four`
 c) `for`

Q7 Errors in the program have been circled.
```
a = "Under
b = "ground"
c = (a - b)
print(a)
```
First error: Missing quotation mark after `"Under`.
Second error: Use of minus symbol instead of addition symbol.
Third error: Variable a is printed instead of c.
The corrected code:
```
a = "Under"
b = "ground"
c = (a + b)
print(c)
Underground
```

Q8
```
01  first = input("Enter your first name: ")
02  second = input("Enter your second name: ")
03  birth = input("Enter your year of birth: ")
04  userOne = first[0:2]
05  userTwo = second[0:3]
06  userName = userOne + userTwo + birth
07  print("Your username is: ",userName)
```
```
Enter your first name: Devveena
Enter your second name: Thulsie
Enter your year of birth: 1984
Your username is: DeThu1984
```

Q9 E.g. Unicode and ASCII

Q10 `chr()` converts code to its character. `ord()` converts a character to its code.

Page 33 — Coding Challenges for Section Three
Head to cgpbooks.co.uk/GCSEPythonExtras to download an example program for each challenge.

Answers

Section Four — Selection

Page 34 — if Statements

Q1 Only `"Have a good day!"` is printed.
Since `"friday" == "Friday"` is False, the code inside the `if` statement isn't executed. Python is case sensitive, which is why `"Friday"` is not considered the same as `"friday"`.

Q2 E.g. Change the `if` statement to: `if day != "Friday"`
The operator has been changed from `==` to `!=`.

Q3 E.g.
```
pizzaDay = input("What day should pizza day be? ")
day = input("What day is it? ")
if day == pizzaDay:
   print("It's pizza time!")
print("Have a good day!")
```

Q4 E.g.
```
day = input("What day is it? ")
if day == "Friday":
   print("It's pizza time!")
   topping1 = input("Enter the first topping: ")
   topping2 = input("Enter the second topping: ")
   topping3 = input("Enter the third topping: ")
   print("Great - you're having a pizza with",
      topping1+", "+topping2+", and "+topping3)
print("Have a good day!")
```
```
What day is it? Friday
It's pizza time!
Enter the first topping: Ham
Enter the second topping: Mushrooms
Enter the third topping: Pineapple
Great - you're having a pizza with Ham, Mushrooms, and Pineapple
Have a good day!
```

Page 36 — else Clause

Q1 E.g.
```
percent = float(input("Enter the percentage: "))

if percent >= 40 and percent <=100:
   print("Test pass.")
else:
   print("Test fail.")
   print("You were",40-percent,"points away.")

print("Goodbye.")
```
```
Enter the percentage: 39
Test fail.
You were 1.0 points away.
Goodbye.
```
If the pupil failed, it means their score was below 40%. To work out how many points away they were, you can subtract their score from 40.

Page 37 — elif Clause

Q1 a)
```
Enter the percentage: 101.9
Grade 9
Goodbye.
```

b)
```
Enter the percentage: Sixty
ValueError: could not convert string to float: 'Sixty'
```
Your answer is also correct if you just wrote 'An error would occur.' `ValueError` occurs as the computer cannot convert `Sixty` (a string) into an integer.

Q2 E.g.
```
percent = float(input("Enter the percentage: "))

if percent < 0 or percent > 100:
   print("This isn't valid.")
elif percent >= 90:
   print("Grade 9")
elif percent >= 80:
   print("Grade 8")
elif percent >= 70:
   print("Grade 7")
elif percent >= 60:
   print("Grade 6")
elif percent >= 50:
   print("Grade 5")
elif percent >= 40:
   print("Grade 4")
elif percent >= 30:
   print("Grade 3")
elif percent >= 20:
   print("Grade 2")
elif percent >= 10:
   print("Grade 1")
else:
   print("Test fail. Sorry.")
print("Goodbye.")
```

Q3 E.g.
```
percent = float(input("Enter the percentage: "))

grade = int(percent/10)

print("Grade",grade)

print("Goodbye.")
```
This is one possible way to do this, although you can't output that it's a failing mark unless you use selection. It'll be outputted as `Grade 0`, not a 'Fail'.

Pages 39-40 — Practice Questions and Activities

Q1 a) E.g. Selection blocks are used to control the flow of a program's execution by making a decision. They are used to set code that should only run if a specific condition has been met. This means that some code within the selection block may not be executed depending on previous conditions.

b) `if` statement

Q2 a)
```
What is your name? Fatima
What year were you born in? 2004
```
Only outputs come from the input prompts. This is because the `print()` line on Line 5 is not executed as the condition was `False`.

Answers

   b) Line 2. The `int` function is trying to cast the input, `2k13`, to an integer. It can't do this without producing a `ValueError` as the `k` prevents it from being converted to a number.

   c) Lines 1 and 2. Line 1 is executed before Line 2 — there's never a change in program flow.

   d) Lines 4 and 5. The program flow will change based on what the condition on Line 4 evaluates to.

   e) The code below has the gaps filled in.

```
06    elif birthYear >= 1995:
07        print(name+", you are a member of Generation Z.")
08    elif birthYear >= 1981:
09        print(name+", you are a Millennial.")
10    else:
11        print("Mmm, I'm not sure what to classify you as...")
```

   f) The first `if` statement's condition is False, so the execution skips line 5 and checks the condition on line 6. This is also False, so the execution moves to line 8. This condition is True, so line 9 is executed. Since one of the previous conditions were True in the block, lines 10 and 11 aren't executed.

Q3 a) `Hi` is printed once. This is because the condition on line 2 is True. `elif`s and `else`s are not checked if a previous condition in the selection block is True — so they are skipped.

   b) `Hi` is printed three times (from lines 3, 5, and 9). Lines 3 and 5 are printed as the conditions after the `if` were True. All `if` statements are checked regardless of what the previous conditions evaluated to, unlike `elif`s. The `else` is part of the block started on line 6. The code on line 9 runs as the `if` statement on line 6 is False.

Q4 a) logic error

   b) The logic error happens because the expressions either side of the Boolean operators aren't full Boolean expressions and will always evaluate to True.
Re-written line (Line 2):
`if ready == "Yes" or ready == "Y" or ready == "y":`

Q5 E.g.
```
if person1 == person2 and person2 == person3:
  print("Wow, what are the odds?")
else:
  print("They aren't all the same.")
```

Page 41 — Coding Challenges for Section Four
Head to cgpbooks.co.uk/GCSEPythonExtras to download an example program for each challenge.

Section Five — Iteration

Pages 42-44 — for Loops

Q1 There are lots of possible answers for this question. Your flowchart should be similar to the one shown on p.42.

Q2
```
for i in range(1,6):
    print(i)
```

Q3 100
75
50
25

Q4 E.g.
```
word = "wheels"
for char in word:
    if char != "e":
        print(char)
```
In the code above the `e` character is skipped using an `if` statement — for a reminder of these take a look at Section Four.

Q5 0
5
10
0
6
12

Q6 There are lots of possible answers for this question. Your program should be similar to the example on p.44.

Page 45 — Practice Questions and Activities

Q1 E.g.

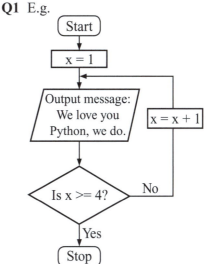

Q2 a) 0
1
2
3
4
5

   b) 10
11
12
13

Answers

Q3 E.g. The third value defines the step size of each iteration. A positive value is an increasing step, a negative value is a decreasing step.

Q4 E.g. A nested `for` loop is when an inner `for` loop is placed inside an outer `for` loop. Each iteration of the outer loop causes the inner loop to run until complete.

Q5 a) `for t in range(4):`
  b) `for s range(1,4):`
  c) Twelve times
  This is because the outer loop iterates 3 times, and for each of those, the inner loop iterates 4 times.
  d) 0 1 2 3 0 2 4 6 0 3 6 9

Q6 Any two benefits, e.g.
- It's quicker to write the code.
- It reduces the likelihood of errors because the code is usually shorter.
- It might save time when checking for errors as there won't be as much code to check.
- It might reduce the time needed to edit the code in the future as you won't need to change the code in multiple places.

Pages 46-48 — while Loops

Q1 There are lots of possible answers for this question. Your flowchart should be similar to the one shown on p.46 but with different text in each box/symbol.
Remember, symbol is just another word for the boxes in flowcharts.

Q2
```
print("Jump on three!")
countdown = 1
while countdown < 4:
    print(countdown)
    countdown = countdown + 1
print("Jump!")
```

Q3 E.g. by adding an `else` clause to the `if` statement.
```
pin = "1977"
while True:
    userPin = input("Enter your 4-digit PIN: ")
    if userPin == pin:
        print("PIN correct, you may proceed.")
        break
    else:
        print("This is incorrect.")
```

Q4 E.g. changing the condition so that it's a 'proper' Boolean expression. This involves moving `input` before the loop and putting the 'correct' message after it.
Remember, != means 'not equals'.
```
pin = "1977"
userPin = input("Enter your 4-digit PIN: ")
while userPin != pin:
    print("This is incorrect.")
    userPin = input("Enter your 4-digit PIN: ")
print("PIN correct, you may proceed.")
```

Q5 E.g.
```
pin = "1977"
for attempt in range(3):
    userPin = input("Enter your 4-digit PIN: ")
    if userPin == pin:
        print("PIN correct, you may proceed.")
        break
else:
    print("You are out of attempts.")
```
As the code will only loop at most 3 times, a `for` loop is a more concise option than a `while` loop here, and `else` works the same with it.

Page 49 — Practice Questions and Activities

Q1 a) `while` loop
  b) A definite loop iterates a set number of times, whereas an indefinite loop will continue until a certain condition is met or broken.

Q2 a) Please enter the current water temperature
  b) The water should now be frozen.

Q3 E.g. Adding an `else` clause to a `while` loop allows there to be code that runs if `break` hasn't been used to end the loop early.

Q4 a) E.g.
```
n = 10
while n > 6:
    n -= 1
    print(n)
```
  b) E.g.
```
n = 9
while n < 13:
    n += 1
    print(n)
```

Q5 E.g.
```
number = 0
while number != 3.142:
    number = float(input("Please enter Pi to three decimal places "))
print("Correct.")
Please enter Pi to three decimal places
3.142
Correct.
```

Page 50 — Coding Challenges for Section Five

Head to cgpbooks.co.uk/GCSEPythonExtras to download an example program for each challenge.

Answers

Section Six — Data Structures

Page 52 — Lists
Q1 integer, float, string and Boolean

Page 53 — Practice Questions and Activities
Q1 Any two valid reasons, e.g.
- To group related items under one name.
- To allow items to easily be stored and recalled at runtime.
- To make code more readable.
- To organise and order data.

Q2 Line 2: `blue`
Line 5: `['red', 'blue', 'purple']`
Line 9: `purple`

Q3 a) Line 1 is trying to index a list called `artists`, but that list isn't initialised until line 2.
b) `Freeman` is passed in to `.index()` as a variable, which doesn't exist. Even if it was a string, a different error would still happen as `Freeman` isn't in the list.

Q4 a) `del planets[3]`
b) `planets.remove("Pluto")`
c) `planets.insert(planets.index("Luyten b") + 1,"Proxima b")`

Q5 E.g.
```
nineTimesTable = []
for i in range(1,11):
    nineTimesTable.append(i*9)
```
There are loads of other ways to do this so don't worry if your program was a bit different.

Page 54 — Iterating Through Lists
Q1
```
band = []

bandSize = int(input("How many members are in the band? "))

for i in range(bandSize):
    userInput = input("Type in a name and then press enter: ")
    band.append(userInput)

print("The band is.... ",end="")

for name in band:
    print(name,end=", ")
```

Q2
```
for i in range(0,len(band),2):
    print(band[i]," (",i+1,"/",len(band),")",sep="",end=", ")
```
The third value in range is the step counter. Making this 2 skips every other index. You need to put in the starting point (0) as the first value, otherwise range() takes the 2 to be the upper limit.

Q3 E.g.
```
band = ["Tariq","Dave","Lucy","George"]

for i in range(len(band)):

    if i != (len(band) - 1):
        print(band[i]," (",i+1,"/",len(band),")",sep="",end=", ")
    else:
        print(band[i]," (",i+1,"/",len(band),")",sep="",end="")
```

Page 56 — 2D Lists
Q1 `[2]`
Q2 `avgTemp[1][2]`
Q3 E.g. Since you know the positions of each item, you can actually remove the inner `for` loop code for this question.

```
register = [['Ahmed','Kolia'],['Angela','Ann','Hamer'],
['Katherine','Kat','Hill'],['Tony','Anderson']]
print("Here are all of the names in the class:")
for i in range(len(register)):
    print(register[i][-2],register[i][-1])
```
The first line of code has been split over two lines here for space. Take a look back at p.30 if you need a reminder about negative indexing.

Page 57 — Practice Questions and Activities
Q1 Line 5 executes five times.
E.g. All items in the `pasta` list are printed because the `if` condition uses Boolean `or`, and all items are either longer than six letters or shorter than nine letters.

Q2 a) `[1][1]`
b) `[3]`
c) `[4][2]`

Q3 E.g. Representing in 2D means a sublist can be used for each event, enabling the date and additional facts to be held as separate items in the sublist. Holding it in a 1D list would make it harder to distinguish between the events, dates and facts.

Q4 a) E.g. In order to access all items in each sublist, both indices should be iterated over. One `for` loop is needed for each.
b) The bug is on line 7.
The upper range of `j` is set to be the length of events, but it should be the length of the sublist (`len(events[i])`). The error occurs when the program tries to index [0][2], which doesn't exist.

Q5 a) The `["A","B","C"]` sublist is added between `["a","b","c"]` and `[1, 2, 3]`.
b) `TypeError`. The indices need to be integers, not strings.

Answers

Page 61 — Practice Questions and Activities

Q1 E.g. The items can't be changed once first initialised.

Q2

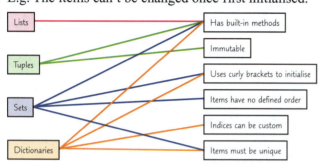

Python dictionaries have been ordered since Python version 3.7. However, they were unordered before that.

Q3 a) {'Sushi', 'Pizza', 'Sandwich', 'Caesar Salad', 'Pasta'}

b) {'Smoothie', 'Water'}

c) E.g. `selection & (basicMains | drinks | snacks)`

Q4 a) E.g. One value is being used to lookup a second value. The actual position of the items isn't important so a numerical index isn't needed.

b) '.uk', '.al', '.co', '.pt', '.ml'

c) E.g. Since `.cn` isn't a key in the dictionary, using it as an index will result in an error. `.get()` will just return `None`.

Page 62 — Coding Challenges for Section Six

Head to cgpbooks.co.uk/GCSEPythonExtras to download an example program for each challenge.

Section Seven — Subroutines

Page 64 — Built-in Subroutines

Q1 3

This is because `^` is symmetric difference, which gives all items except those that are in both. 2 and -7 are in both, so, despite being less than 3, they are excluded.

Q2 E.g.

```
# Using max() with a list
items = [5,100,55,23,300]
currentMax = items[0]
for item in items:
    if item > currentMax:
        currentMax = item
print(currentMax)
```
```
300
```

```
# Using max() with variables
a = 5000
b = 500
c = 50
if a > b and a > c:
    print(a)
elif b > a and b > c:
    print(b)
else:
    print(c)
```
```
5000
```

```
# Using max() with a dictionary
items = {5:"a",10:"b",3:"c"}
currentMax = list(items.keys())[0]
for key in items.keys():
    if key > currentMax:
        currentMax = key
print(currentMax)
```
```
10
```

In the above code, the initialisation of `currentMax` before the loop could have been `currentMax = 0`, although that's assuming that the keys are positive. If all the keys weren't positive, then 0 would remain the `currentMax` throughout which would be incorrect.

Page 66 — Practice Questions and Activities

Q1 Any two valid reasons, e.g.
- To avoid repetitive code.
- To make a program more efficient.

Q2 a) Any two valid functions, e.g. `int()` and `ord()`.

b) Any two valid methods, e.g. `.lower()` and `.count()`

Answers

Q3 Any two valid differences, e.g.
- Methods have a full stop before the method name and functions don't.
- Methods can change an object directly whereas the result of a function needs to be assigned to an object to change it.
- Methods always act on an object (the thing before the '.') where as functions don't - they are just called by their name.

Q4 a) `print(max(x,y,z))`
b) `print(min(j,k,l))`
c) `[1, 7, 13, 20, 325, 980]`

Q5 a)

Function	Procedure	Method
int	print	append
input		join
str		

b) The `n1` variable is first added to the `fibonacci` list as a string. The `nth` term is calculated by adding the two previous terms (`n1` and `n2`) before they're updated, so `n1` is the old `n2` and `n2` is now `nth`. `count` then increments by 1. If this is smaller than `terms`, the `while` loop iterates again.

Page 68 — User-defined Functions

Q1 Any two valid reasons, e.g.
- It would save the company time when employing new staff.
- It would save the company time in the future if the format of their ID codes changes. They would just need to change the function definition for the changes to be applied to the whole program.

Q2 Old MacDonald had a farm
ee-aye, ee-aye, oh!
And on that farm he had a dog
ee-aye, ee-aye, oh!

Page 69 — Practice Questions and Activities

Q1 E.g. Functions are defined at the beginning of a program so that they can then be used throughout the rest of the program.

Q2 E.g. These are Python keywords that already have defined meanings. Defining your own functions with their names would lead to errors.

Q3 E.g. The menu hasn't been called in the main program because of the indentation. Brackets are also missing in the calling statement.

Q4 a)
```
def goldilocks():
    porridge = "hot"
    print(porridge)
goldilocks()
```
The error was caused by the function being called before it was defined.

b)
```
def get_postCode():
    postCode = input("Enter postcode")
    print(postCode)
get_postCode()
```
It's the missing colon in line 1 that causes the error in this program.

c)
```
def twelve():
    for i in range(1,11):
        print(12*i)
twelve()
```
Note the added indentation inside the definition.

Q5 E.g. Line 1 is executed first, and then Line 3's definition is acknowledged by Python, but the program skips to execute line 7. Line 7 calls the function, so the flow returns to Line 3 and the function is executed. When Line 5 finishes, the execution returns to Line 7. Finally, Line 8 is executed.

Page 73 — Practice Questions and Activities

Q1 E.g. A global variable is assigned outside all function definitions / in the main program and it can be accessed by the whole program. A local variable is assigned inside a function definition and can only be accessed by that function.

Q2 a) The variable v is only initialised within the function (so is local) which means it can't be used within the main program.

b) The line w = w / 5 assigns a local variable w but to do w / 5 it needs to use the current value of w. Despite there being a global w, as there's a local w an UnboundLocalError occurs. This problem can be fixed by adding a "global w" statement within the function.
The returned value of w hasn't been held in a variable in the main program, but that doesn't cause the error.

Q3 a) and b)

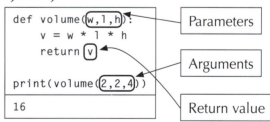

Q4 E.g. To pass in data from the main program to be used inside the function. They help avoid the need to use global variables.

Answers

Q5 E.g.
```
def triangle(h, b):
    return (h * b) / 2

print(triangle(10,5))
25.0
```
The empty line before the `print()` line isn't necessary for the program to work — it's there to make the program easier to read.

Page 74 — Modules
Q1 E.g.
```
import math
def area(radius):
    return math.floor(math.pi * radius ** 2)
print(area(10))
```
See p.23 if you need a reminder on how to use '**'. The value '10' has been used as an example to show how the program works — any other value would also be correct.

Page 75 — The Time Module
Q1 E.g.
```
import time
q1 = input("Hi there, how are you today?")
time.sleep(2)
print("Thank you for sharing.")
time.sleep(2)
print("To be honest, I feel exactly the same.")
```

Page 76 — The Random Module
Q1
```
import random
choice = random.randint(-9,9)
print(choice)
```

Q2 E.g.
```
import random
import time

def bank():
    question = input("Ask me your question ")

def response(answer):
    r1 = "Definitely"
    r2 = "Maybe, maybe not"
    r3 = "No way, not on my watch"
    r4 = "Watch the stars"
    r5 = "Anything is possible"
    r6 = "Only time will tell"
    r7 = "Go for it I say"
    r8 = "Literally no"

    print("Let me think...")
    time.sleep(3)
    if answer == 1:
        print(r1)
    elif answer == 2:
        print(r2)
    elif answer == 3:
        print(r3)
    elif answer == 4:
        print(r4)
    elif answer == 5:
        print(r5)
    elif answer == 6:
        print(r5)
    elif answer == 7:
        print(r5)
    elif answer == 8:
        print(r5)
    else:
        print("Error")

bank()
response (random.randint(1,8))

bank()
response (random.randint(1,8))
```

Pages 77-78 — Turtle Graphics
Q1 There are lots of possible answers for this question. Make sure to test your code in Python and make any corrections you need to if you make a wrong turn.

Answers

Q2 E.g.

```
from turtle import *

fillcolor("yellow")
begin_fill()
for t in range(5):
    fd(80)
    rt(120)
    fd(80)
    rt(-48)
end_fill()

penup()
goto(200,0)
pendown()

fillcolor("blue")
begin_fill()
for t in range(3):
    fd(150)
    rt(-120)
end_fill()
```

The first shape is drawn, the turtle moves to a new location without drawing anything, then it starts drawing the second shape from there.

The example code above uses the blue triangle and yellow star from page 78 but you can use any combination of shapes from the page.

Page 79 — Practice Questions and Activities

Q1 There are many possible answers, e.g.
- random — to generate random numbers to be used within programs.
- math — a range of mathematical tools.
- time — incorporates the passage and calculation of time within programs.

Q2 an epoch

Q3 It will display the current local date and time.

Q4 E.g.
```
num1 = int(input("Number 1:"))
num2 = int(input("Number 2:"))
import random
choice = random.randint(num1,num2)
print("I'll give you the number",choice)
```

Q5 a) E.g.
```
from turtle import *
fillcolor("red")
begin_fill()
for t in range(3):
    fd(150)
    rt(-120)
end_fill()
```

b) E.g.
```
from turtle import *
fillcolor("green")
begin_fill()
fd(20)
lt(90)
fd(60)
rt(90)
fd(20)
lt(90)
fd(20)
lt(90)
fd(60)
lt(90)
fd(20)
lt(90)
fd(20)
rt(90)
fd(60)
end_fill()
```

c) E.g.
```
from turtle import *
pencolor("yellow")
for t in range(6):
    fd(60)
    lt(60)
```

Page 80 — Coding Challenges for Section Seven

Head to cgpbooks.co.uk/GCSEPythonExtras to download an example program for each challenge.

Answers

Section Eight — File Handling

Page 86 — Updating and Deleting Content in Text Files

Q1 E.g.
```
with open("jobDetails.csv","r+") as file:
    fileContents = file.readlines()
    for i in range(1,len(fileContents)):
        if "CEO" in fileContents[i]:
            newLine = "CEO,Oversees the
            company,142000\n"
            fileContents[i] = newLine
    file.seek(0)
    file.truncate()
    file.write("".join(fileContents))
```

Page 87 — Practice Questions and Activities

Q1 E.g. To enable data to be permanently stored. It also means that data wouldn't be lost when the program closes or power is lost. External files allow data to be loaded into a program, e.g. with computer game progress.

Q2 The random module is being imported. Then a file called 'pythonFacts.txt' is read and the lines are held as a list called `allFacts`. The number of items in the list (4) is printed. Line 7 uses a random index to print a random item from the list. The `.strip()` method prevents a newline character being printed. The file connection is then terminated.

Q3 a) ./Other Files/Europe.csv
  b) ./Other Files/Data/Asia.csv
  c) ../South America.txt

Q4 The answers have been highlighted.
```
import time

with open("usageLog.txt", "a") as file:
    timestamp = time.ctime()
    file.write(timestamp + "\n")
```

Q5 E.g. You first need to read the data from the external text file. You may need to parse this depending on what you are changing. Within the program you then make the change, and then write back all of the data to the original file. You should make sure this data is in the same format as it was at the beginning.

Page 88 — Coding Challenges

Head to cgpbooks.co.uk/GCSEPythonExtras to download an example program for each exercise.

Section Nine — Making Programs Robust

Page 91 — Regular Expressions

Q1 E.g.
```
import re

text = "mississippi"
x = re.findall("i",text)
print(x)

['i', 'i', 'i', 'i']
```

Page 93 — Practice Questions and Activities

Q1 Any three valid checks, e.g.
- Check the length.
- Check it falls within the expected value range.
- Check it's in the correct format.

Q2
```
wordEntry = input("Please enter a six letter word:")
wordLength = 6
while len(wordEntry)!= wordLength:
    wordEntry = input("Please try again:")
print("Word accepted, thank you")
```

Q3 E.g. The user input is being cast to an integer in line 1. The `int` function only works with whole numbers, so any input which isn't a whole number will cause an error. Validating the input using `.isdigit()` before it's cast could prevent the error.

Q4 E.g. Regular expressions are used to check if a specific pattern of characters is contained in a string.

Q5 E.g. They can be used to replace unknown characters in a search string.

Q6 a) E.g. To validate an amount of money.
  b) The £ is part of the string. The . has a \ before it because it needs to be escaped as it's also a wildcard. The {2} indicates that two digits are required for the pence.
  c) E.g.

	Normal	Boundary	Erroneous
Examples	£5.55, £1022.99, £0.44	£0.00, £9.99	50 pence, Hello!, 10.222
Is it correctly validated by the program?	Yes	Yes	Yes

Page 94 — Debugging

Q1
```
x = 3
y = 1
prinnt("There are",X+y,errors in this program"(
```
Error 1: `print` spelt incorrectly.
Error 2: Capital X variable should be lowercase.
Error 3: Missing quotation mark before errors.
Error 4: Incorrect end bracket.

Answers

Page 96 — Exception Handling

Q1
```
x = int(input("Please enter first number:"))
y = int(input("Please enter second number:"))
try:
    z = x/y
    print(z)
except ZeroDivisionError:
    print("The second value cannot be zero")
```

Q2 E.g. The use of the `//` operator rounds the number down to the nearest integer whereas the `/` operator would generate a float.

Page 97 — Practice Questions and Activities

Q1 E.g. The process of removing errors (bugs) from lines of code.

Q2 Errors in the program have been circled.

```
%random number generator
inport random
num = random.ranint(0,100)
print(numb)
```

Line 1 error: `%` instead of `#` symbol used for a comment
Line 2 error: `inport` should be spelled `import`
Line 3 error: `random.ranint` should be `random.randint`
Line 4 error: `numb` should be `num`

Q3 E.g. The program will run one line at a time, allowing errors to be spotted easily.

Q4 a) The `print()` on line 1 is executed and the outer `while` loop begins. As 7 is a valid integer, line 5 can cast it without an error. It's within the range specified in the inner `while` loop and so just the break statement is run, ending the outer `while` loop. No exceptions were raised so lines 9 to 13 are skipped. The final `print()` is run.

b) The beginning is the same as when 7 was typed in. However, since four can't be cast to an integer, line 5 raises a `ValueError` exception. The rest of the code inside try is skipped. Only the `ValueError` specific except block is run, with the `print()` on line 13 being shown. The outer `while` loop then iterates, asking for another input. A `KeyboardInterrupt` exception is raised when the user tries to abort the program while it's running, usually with CTRL + C. Catching this exception prevents them from doing this.

Q5 E.g. One generic `except` block applies to all exceptions, and so it's hard to make the error message useful enough for the user or developer to understand what went wrong. Catching specific exceptions means more precise messages can be outputted. Also, the next step to recover from the exception may vary depending on what the exception was.

Page 98 — Coding Challenges for Section Nine

Head to cgpbooks.co.uk/GCSEPythonExtras to download an example program for each challenge.

Section Ten — Algorithms and More Coding Challenges

Lots of the answers in this section are in Python files which can be downloaded from cgpbooks.co.uk/GCSEPythonExtras.

Pages 99-100 — Searching Algorithms

Q1 An example answer can be found in the file named:
S10-p99-SearchingAlgorithms-Q1-Answer
A linear search starts at the beginning of the list and checks every item one by one. It continues until the target is found or the end of the list is reached.

Q2 An example answer can be found in the file named:
S10-p99-SearchingAlgorithms-Q2-Answer

Q3 An example answer can be found in the file named:
S10-p100-SearchingAlgorithms-Q3-Answer
It's easier to do this if you don't actually change the original list — so instead of trying to discard parts, define start and end variables and use these to represent the changing list.

Pages 101-103 — Sorting Algorithms

Q1 An example answer can be found in the file named:
S10-p101-SortingAlgorithms-Q1-Answer

Q2 An example answer can be found in the file named:
S10-p101-SortingAlgorithms-Q2-Answer

Q3 An example answer can be found in the file named:
S10-p102-SortingAlgorithms-Q3-Answer

Q4 An example answer can be found in the file named:
S10-p103-SortingAlgorithms-Q4-Answer

Q5 An example answer can be found in the file named:
S10-p103-SortingAlgorithms-Q5-Answer

Page 104 — Practice Questions and Activities

Q1 a) linear search
This is because it goes through each item in turn.

b) `Green found at index 3`

c) The not equals sign has been used (`!=`). Fix by using `==` instead.
There is a missing `)` on the last line, but this is a syntax, not logic, error.

d) E.g. The algorithm will continue looping through the list even once the target has been found, which is wasteful. Possible improvements include using `break` or having a `while` loop instead of the `for` loop.
You only need to give one improvement in your answer.

Q2 E.g.
- The outer `for` loop will continue to loop unnecessarily if an earlier pass had no swaps. You could either use `break` or replace it with a `while` loop with a boolean flag (e.g. `cleanPass`).
- The inner `for` loop does not need to consider the last n items if n passes have been done already (as those items have been 'bubbled' to the end already). The upper range limit can therefore be adjusted based on the number of passes done already.

Answers

Q3 a) insertion sort

b) [91, 14, 7, 4, 1]

c) E.g. The subroutine calls itself in the final `if` statement. After one item has been added to the sorted partition, the recursion is used to insert the next item into the sorted partition (which is why the argument is `index + 1`).

Q4 E.g.
- If the list is unsorted, they could adapt linear search so that each item is checked and compared to the current biggest and smallest values.
- If the list is sorted, they can index the first and last item to find the smallest and largest value, respectively.
- If the list is big (which this one is likely to be) and unsorted, it may be more efficient to apply a sorting algorithm to it as it may still be quicker than the adapted linear search. Merge sort is the most time efficient option.

Pages 105-109 — Advanced Coding Challenges

The answers provided here are example programs — for longer coding challenges like these there are usually many different ways to solve them so you might've gone about the challenge in a different way. If you're really stuck getting started with a challenge, you could take a look at the example program or experiment with it first before trying to make the whole program yourself.

C1 Snowman guessing game — an example answer can be found in the file named: S10-p105-LongerCodingChallenges-Ch1-Snowman
The file dictionary.txt should be used with this program.

C2 Denary-binary converter — an example answer can be found in the file named: S10-p106-LongerCodingChallenges-Ch2-DenaryBinaryConverter

C3 Mersenne primes — an example answer can be found in the file named: S10-p106-LongerCodingChallenges-Ch3-MersennePrimes
When dealing with large prime numbers and big exponents, calculations can be slow even for a modern computer unless you code efficiently.
The Lucas-Lehmer test is an example of a clever algorithm that can bypass doing a lot of unnecessary steps. If your Mersenne primes code is slow and you're having trouble implementing this test, the following pseudocode may help:

```
SUBROUTINE Lucas-Lehmer(P):
# The first term
    S = 4
# The possible Mersenne prime being tested
    M = 2^P - 1
# Keep going until you reach S_(P-2)
    FOR i = 1 TO P - 2
        S = (S² - 2) MOD M
# At the end, if S_(P-2) = 0 then it's a
# Mersenne prime
    IF S = 0 THEN
        OUTPUT M
    ELSE
        OUTPUT "Not a Mersenne prime"
```

You can then test this function with different values of P (as long as they are greater than 2).

C4 Run-length encoding — an example answer can be found in the file named: S10-p107-LongerCodingChallenges-Ch4-RunLengthEncoding

C5 Turtle graphics cityscape — an example answer can be found in the file named: S10-p107-LongerCodingChallenges-Ch5-TurtleGraphicsCityscape
There are loads of different solutions to this challenge — the example program is just one possibility.

C6 Vigenère cipher — an example answer can be found in the file named: S10-p108-LongerCodingChallenges-Ch6-VigenereCipher

C7 Breaking Vigenère — The decrypted words and key can be found in a comment in the example answer. This example answer can be found in the file named: S10-p109-LongerCodingChallenges-Ch7-BreakingVigenere
Hint: you can sneakily use the decrypt algorithm to output a possible key. Normally, you decrypt ciphertext with the key to give the plaintext. Here, as you don't know what this key is yet, you can instead decrypt the ciphertext with a possible plaintext. This will instead give you a possible key, which you can then try out on the other ciphertext.
You can use vigenereWords.txt to test your program.

C8 Lottery draw — an example answer can be found in the file named: S10-p109-LongerCodingChallenges-Ch8-Lottery Draw
You can use lotteryDraw.txt to test your program.

C9 Frequency analysis — an example answer can be found in the file named: S10-p109-LongerCodingChallenges-Ch9-FrequencyAnalysis
You can use romeoAndJuliet.txt to test your program.

Index

A
algorithms 9
.append() 52, 65
arithmetic operators 23
ASCII 30, 107
 art 20, 105
assignment 13, 14, 21, 65, 70
assignment operators 47

B
backslashes 18
binary 27, 81
binary search 100
boolean
 data type 21
 operators 27, 28, 35
boundary data 89
break 48
bubble sort 101
bugs 67, 94

C
calling 63, 64, 67, 72
camel case 14
casting 22, 64, 96
clauses 36
.close() 82
commas (as separators) 18
comments 12
concatenation 18, 30
condition-controlled
  loops 46-48
constants 58, 71, 74
.count() 29, 58
count-controlled loops 43, 44
CSV files 83

D
data structures 51-60
data types 21, 22
debugging 5, 94
declarations 71
defensive programming 89
definite loops 43
dictionaries 51, 60, 64, 65
div 23
drawing using turtle 77, 78

E
editor window (IDLE) 5
elif 37, 38
else 36-38, 48
epoch 75
erroneous data 89
errors 6-8
 logic 6, 38, 47, 68, 85
 syntax 6, 7
escape characters 18, 92
except blocks 95, 96
exception handling 95, 96
exponentiation 23
external files 81-86
extreme data 89

F
.findall() 91, 92
float() 22, 64
floats 21, 22
flowcharts 8-10, 35, 42, 46, 63
for loops 43, 44, 54, 60
functions
 built-in 64, 65
 user-defined 67, 68

G
.get() 60, 65
global variables 70-72
Graphical User Interface (GUI) 110

H
hash symbols 12
highlighting 12, 94

I
IDEs (Integrated Development Environments) 3
IDLE 3-5
 editor window 5
 shell window 4, 5
if statements 34-38
immutable 58, 60
indefinite loops 46-48

indentation 5, 34, 35
.index() 52, 58
indexing 30, 51, 52, 54-56
infinite loops 47
initialisation 13, 14
inner loops 44
input() 16, 17, 64
.insert() 52
insertion sort 102
installing Python 3
integers 21, 22
invalid data 89
.isalpha() 90
.isdigit() 90
.items() 60
iteration 42-48, 54

J
.join() 86

K
.keys() 60
key-value pairs 60
keywords 67

L
len() 29, 56, 64, 90
linear search 99
lists 51, 52, 54
 2D 55, 56, 85
local variables 70, 71
logic errors 6, 38, 47, 68, 85
lowerCamelCase 14

M
main memory 81
math module 74
max() 64
merge sort 102, 103
methods 52, 65
min() 64
MOD 23

Index

modules 74
   math 74
   OS 84
   pdb 94
   random 76
   re 91, 92
   time 75
   turtle 77, 78
Monty Python 2

N
nesting 38, 44, 56, 95
normal data 89

O
operators 23-28
   arithmetic 23
   assignment 47
   boolean 27, 28, 35
   relational 26
   set 59
OS module 84
outer loops 44

P
parameters 72
parsing 83
penguin 99
pi 74
pivot 100
plain text 82
print() 12, 64
procedures 65
program design cycle 11
prompts 16
pseudocode 10, 103

R
random access memory (RAM) 81
random module 76
range() 43, 44, 54, 90
.readline() 83
read mode 82

regular expressions 91, 92
relational operators 26
.remove() 52
reserved words 67
return values 72
robustness 44, 89, 90, 94, 95
runtime 7, 12, 17

S
scope 70, 71
.search() 91, 92
searching algorithms 99, 100
.seek() 86,
selection 34-38
separators 18
sequence 34
sets 59
shell window (IDLE) 4, 5
.sleep() 75
snake case 14
sorted() 65
sorting algorithms 101-103
.split() 83
str() 64
string handling 29, 30
strings 21, 29, 30
.strip() 83
.sub() 91
subroutines 9, 63-74
   built-in 64, 65, 72
   user-defined 67, 68
syntax errors 6, 7

T
test data 89
testing 8, 11, 89, 94
text files 82, 83, 85, 86
.time() 75
time module 75
.truncate() 86
try...except 95, 96
tuples 58
turtle graphics 77, 78

U
Unicode 30
.upper() 65
UpperCamelCase 14
user-defined functions 67, 68

V
validation 89, 90, 92, 95
.values() 60
variables 4, 7, 13, 14, 17
   global 70-72
   local 70, 71
   naming rules 14
volatile memory 81

W
while loops 46-48
wildcards 92
.write() 85
write mode 85